MARCO  POLO
NEW YORK

with Local Tips

*The author's special recommendations are
highlighted in yellow throughout this guide*

There are five symbols to help you find your way around this guide:

Marco Polo's top recommendations — the best in each category

sites with a scenic view

where the local people meet

where young people get together

(100/A1)
pages and coordinates for the street atlas
(O) *outside area covered by the street atlas*

MARCO ⊕ POLO

Travel guides and language guides in this series:

Algarve • Amsterdam • Australia • Berlin • Brittany • California
Channel Islands • Costa Brava/Barcelona • Costa del Sol/Granada
Côte d'Azur • Crete • Cuba • Cyprus • Eastern USA • Florence • Florida
Gran Canaria • Greek Islands/Aegean • Ibiza • Ireland • Istanbul • Lanzarote
London • Mallorca • Malta • New York • New Zealand • Normandy • Paris
Prague • Rhodes • Rome • Scotland • South Africa • Southwestern USA
Tenerife • Turkish Coast • Tuscany • Venice • Western Canada

French • German • Italian • Spanish

*Marco Polo would be very interested to hear your
comments and suggestions. Please write to:*

North America:
Marco Polo North America
70 Bloor Street East
Oshawa, Ontario, Canada
(B) 905-436-2525

United Kingdom:
World Leisure Marketing Ltd
Marco Polo Guides
Newmarket Drive
Derby DE24 8NW

*2nd revised edition 1999
© Mairs Geographischer Verlag, Ostfildern, Germany
Author: Doris Chevron
Translation: Georgina Simpson
English edition 1999: Gaia Text
Editorial director: Ferdinand Ranft
Chief editor: Marion Zorn
Cartography Street Atlas: © Hallwag AG, Bern
Design and layout: Thienhaus/Wippermann
Printed in Germany*

CONTENTS

Discover New York

*The capital of wealth, entertainment
and the American Dream*

'New York, New York ... I wanna wake up in the city that doesn't sleep.' Countless songs have been written extolling the virtues of the great metropolis. In a few simple but heartfelt words, Frank Sinatra's timeless hit evokes the extraordinary zest for life this dynamic city possesses and expresses the fascination it holds for both those who live there and those who dream of going there: it is the capital city of the American Dream.

Although the streets and landmarks of New York are familiar to most of us from film and television, the only way to really understand this restless and thriving city, and the strength of its influence on the rest of the world, is to experience it first hand – 'to wake up in the city that doesn't sleep' to the sound of honking horns, the constant hum of traffic and wailing sirens, and to venture out into the thick of New York street life.

*South Street Seaport:
where yachts, tall ships and
racing boats moor side by side*

No other city in the world can profess to being more ruthless than New York and yet, paradoxically, people develop a very sentimental attachment to the place. It tends to have one of two very opposite effects on its visitors. They are either completely enthralled by it or else very put off by it, but those who leave the city with fond memories and a desire to return far outnumber those who don't. It's difficult not to be mesmerized by its incredible diversity and vitality. Lying at the mouth of the Hudson River in all its sprawling grandeur, New York leaves an unforgettable impression. It is a place where even the most mundane and everyday things can be fascinating.

'New York, New York, so good they named it twice ...' New York City, New York State – the name of a town is rarely mentioned in America without the name of the state being uttered in the same breath, a custom that dates back to the time before postcodes were introduced (Paris, Texas; Boston, Massachusetts; Denver, Colorado). Despite its prominence on the

The Statue of Liberty: a gift from France to the New World

world map, however, New York has never been regarded as a political stronghold or as a showpiece of cultural and historical splendour. The last significant historical event that took place here was in April 1776, when Commander of the American Forces, George Washington, temporarily set up his headquarters on the Hudson River during the War of Independence from British colonialism. Even when the United Nations set up its main headquarters in New York after World War II, the political vacuum still persisted. Governed by politicians far away in Washington and in the small state capital Albany, New York remains at a distance and rather impervious to it all. It is not a city that lives and breathes through its own history. It is a modern city in a state of constant flux and regeneration, a city that lives very much in the present, thriving off the energy of its people, the dynamics of money, the pressure of immense competition and the pursuit of success.

Once the world's largest city, the population of New York has long since been exceeded by those of Mexico City and Tokyo. Today the city's inhabitants number seven million – or 25 million if you count the whole of the Metropolitan Area, which encompasses neighbouring districts such as Long Island, Westchester County, New Jersey and Connecticut. Many of the working population commute to the heart of the city, Manhattan. Every year, approximately 31 million visitors descend upon Manhattan. Even though one third of the city's economy is derived from tourism, New York pays no special attention to its tourists. Life is lived very much in the fast lane and the interests of those wishing to meander along the streets and take in the sights at a leisurely pace are not well catered for within the massive grid of street blocks. There are only a few havens of peace and quiet where you can take a break from the fray: the square in the middle of the Rockefeller Center, the steps of St. Patrick's Cathedral on Fifth Avenue, or those at the Metropolitan Museum being the main options. And, because of the lack of alternatives, these places tend to get very crowded.

Needless to say, money is the driving force behind all this relentless activity. Here, more than anywhere else in America, the almighty 'greenback' reigns supreme. New York is the undisputed capital of trade and commerce: it is a hectic, loud, challenging, merciless and powerful place. So powerful, in fact, that when Wall Street sneezes, the stock exchanges in Tokyo, Frankfurt and London all catch a cold. Manhattan is not an industrial centre, but a control centre. It is the place where affairs are managed and buttons pressed. As the media capital of the USA, New York is the centre of information and popular culture. This information is dispersed across the rest of the United States via huge television and radio networks and massively circulated national newspapers and magazines. All the major publishing companies, record companies and music publishers have their head offices in the city and operate from here with their sights set firmly on the world markets. But the world markets are as demanding as the Americans are hard-working. New York really is 'the city that doesn't sleep'. The peace that descends in the small hours is short-lived. It is soon shattered with the din of dustbins being emptied on every corner and streets being cleaned, heralding the start of another hectic working day for the vast army of white- and blue-collar workers.

But even when business stops for the day and offices close in the evenings, the city continues to pulsate with activity. Curtains rise across the world's greatest entertainment centre. Every evening you can catch film premières, musicals, ballet performances, plays and operas, or seek out the throb of the countless clubs. The New York audience, however, while enthusiastic, is exacting and highly critical. Sinatra's words ring especially true for those trying to further their career in the performing arts: 'if [you] can make it there, [you'd] make it anywhere'.

In the city that never sleeps, you can shop, watch TV, visit bars, have fun and be entertained 24 hours a day, seven days a week, every day of the year: there are no compulsory closing times or restricted overtime. Boredom is not a word in the New York vocabulary. It's not the ideal place to come if you want to just sit back, absorb impressions and contemplate life, but all the activity is infectious. You'll find that you have plenty of energy and enthusiasm for exploring the city.

It's very easy to find your way around Manhattan. Built on a grid system, the streets are straight and clearly numbered. Many of the major sights are clustered together around the same area, or separated by just a few blocks, which means it's easy to explore the city on foot. That said, it's a good idea to familiarize yourself a little with the city before you arrive. It isn't advisable for newcomers just to roam around aimlessly. If you don't know where you're going, you could be taking risks wandering into dangerous streets or high-risk areas of the city.

New York is a city of extreme and harsh contrasts. Winters are dry and icy cold, summers are hot (temperatures can reach up to 35°C/95°F) and humid. Central Park is a haven in the midst of the urban jungle, a breathing space in between the heavy, endless blocks of concrete. Churches, which in any other town would soar above the surrounding buildings, are dwarfed by skyscrapers. While New York's rich display their wealth and enjoy the economic boom of the 1990s and the radical retreat of criminality, the homeless and disabled with their outstretched hands document the all too real existing poverty. The destitute are everywhere – modern-day outcasts for whom the way back into the social system remains harshly blocked. New York is expensive. Those who are unemployed and can't pay their rent will fall with frightening rapidity into the social void. Begging is the last alternative before stealing, and fewer and fewer are shrinking away from this prospect. It's a sad but inescapable fact, so be warned: tourists are an easy target.

Between the juxtaposition of wealth and poverty, great and small, old and new, there is astonishing diversity. Every race, nation and creed can be found in New York. In the words of

Quentin Crisp, 'when you are in this city, you feel you are at the heart of the world'. The majority who emigrated here, have made their homes here for political or economic reasons. Driven by hope for a better future, at least for their children, they each brought with them a piece of their homeland. In this way, many traditions live on in New York, even if they are sometimes hidden from view.

Even today, the population of New York is in a state of constant flux. During the last century, many Europeans from Ireland, Germany, Austria and Russia em-igrated to America, thus altering the traditionally English-speaking environment. At the beginning of this century,

Wall Street is the nerve-centre of the financial world

immigrants from Italy and Poland began to arrive in droves. Then, when the Nazis came to power in Germany, and during World War II, New York became a safe haven for Jews fleeing Europe to escape persecution and death. They all came to America by ship, and their first sight of the new land of freedom was of course the Statue of Liberty. These new citizens found themselves in a growing metropolis with a healthy economy. They keenly adopted a pioneering spirit, and many of them were rewarded with great wealth.

A multifaceted unity has thus emerged. New York City has a unique racial mix not found anywhere else in the U.S., or the world for that matter. With millions of Spanish-speaking immigrants from Central and South America, with hundreds of thousands of Chinese, Koreans and Vietnamese, and with the influx of many black Americans from the American South, the city, although beginning to lose its integrative abilities, is still a simmering melting pot.

In 1989 a historic precedent was set by the electorate when democrat David Dinkins was voted the first black mayor of New York. He declared with pride that: 'New York is no longer a melting pot. It is a mosaic in which each part is of equal value.' But there are cracks appearing in the mosaic. If you look at the five boroughs, each one is like a separate city (as they were prior to 1898 when they were amalgamated to create Greater New York). After Manhattan, Brooklyn would be the fourth largest city in the USA; Queens would have two of the largest airports in the United States – John F. Kennedy and La Guardia; the Bronx boasts one of the country's best zoos and the great New York Yankees base-ball stadium. But what would become of these boroughs if they were independent of one another? The Bronx is the poor-house of New York and a hotspot for drug-related crime, while Staten Island, the fifth

The Financial District, Manhattan

10

borough, across the wide bay, is like a ship with no captain, a poor sleepy backwater town, ever dependent upon its lifelines to Manhattan, which not only carries the massive weight of the skyscrapers on its back, but also bears the economic responsibility of the entire city.

Manhattan began to develop slowly around its southernmost tip and then spread rapidly northwards. When every piece of land had been built upon, the town stopped building outwards and began to build upwards. Even the Manhattan sky has run out of space. Old houses are constantly disappearing and being replaced by newer, wider, taller ones. Buildings in the process of being renovated or rebuilt are a common sight and that's why, with the exception of Greenwich Village, you'll see very few, if any, streets lined with old houses. There are only a smattering left of the grand old townhouses and the once very popular five-storey houses (brownstones). Land is the most expensive thing you can buy in Manhattan as it's the scarcest commodity. Wherever money is no longer flowing because economic development has rigorously set a new course, whole areas lie abandoned, and only when they have been torn down and replaced with something bigger and better are they of renewed interest to investors.

Over the past few years, students, artists and musicians, in their constant search for cheap accommodation, have been moving into the underdeveloped parts of the city, gradually transforming what were originally run-down areas into desirable places to live. These areas soon become 'in' places and the inevitable gentrification ensues. No sooner has an area acquired a new look, than up pop shops, restaurants, galleries and hotels. This then leads to higher prices, which force out the students and artists who can no longer afford to live there. In this way, over the last few years, the faces of downtown Manhattan, Greenwich Village, SoHo, TriBeCa and the East Village have been changed by spectacular developments.

The city's inhabitants, however, are beginning to value their architectural heritage. Efforts to prevent the traces of New York's history from disappearing down the tube have been stepped up. One of the most striking examples of this was the renovation of the Statue of Liberty on the occasion of its centenary in 1986. This project was predominantly funded by private donations, as is much of the upkeep of New York's cultural heritage. Millions of dollars flow continually into the Metropolitan Museum. Influential residents, like the millionairess Brooke Astor, organize fund-raising galas for the super rich, which finance such huge conservation projects as the renovation of the Public Library on Fifth Avenue. Private funds achieve what public authorities, with their dwindling resources, do not have the power to do.

New York is steeped in art and culture of the highest degree and anyone who visits the city can reap the benefits of the generosity of these rich patrons who have filled the city's cultural coffers to the full.

Exploring the city

The Empire State Building, SoHo, Staten Island Ferry, Central Park and Broadway – experience the thrill of seeing all the legendary sights, so familiar from TV and films

Exploring a city like New York is both exhilarating and exhausting. There is so much to take in, so many wonderful things to see and experience, that it can be quite overwhelming. New York boasts some of the boldest architecture within the smallest space: the highest skyscrapers, the largest bridges, the most impressive churches and in the midst of it all, a public park almost twice the size of Monaco.

Most of this architectural development grew at lightning speed and the majority of the buildings do not yet exceed in age the average human lifespan. Architects design buildings that often stand in stark contrast to one another, the emphasis being on utility rather than beauty and harmony. Older buildings were forced to give way to the new and were demolished beyond salvation, simply because they were lying on scarce and precious land. It is only in the last few years that a number of poli-

ticians and influential citizens have developed an awareness and respect for history, classifying whole areas over a century old as conservation areas of special historical significance (the prime example being the Upper West Side). This awareness unfortunately came about too late to save many buildings, but for those houses built in the 20th century there is still hope. The best place to get an overall view of the city is from the top of the Empire State Building. It is easy to make out from here the group of islands upon which New York is built, the grid-like network of Manhattan's streets with its wide avenues running from north to south, Central Park and the awesome skyscrapers. You can pick out Downtown and Uptown, West Side and East Side and the borders of the five boroughs: Manhattan, Brooklyn, Queens, the Bronx and Staten Island. The best way of getting from A to B is on foot or by subway if you want to cover long distances quickly. A boat trip around Manhattan is particularly recommended.

Rockefeller Center: the golden Prometheus

ARCHITECTURAL HIGHLIGHTS & MONUMENTS

Brooklyn Bridge (115/D4)
★ Construction work on the first bridge that joined Manhattan with the then separate city of Brooklyn, under the direction of German-born engineer John Augustus Roebling and his son, was completed in 1883 after 15 years. The two towers soar to a height of 89 m (294 ft) amid hundreds of steel cables. The completed bridge, spanning 530 m (1750 ft) over the East River, was hailed as the 'eighth wonder of the world'. A walkway stretches beneath its neo-Gothic arches, making an ideal vantage point for pedestrians to enjoy the view of Manhattan's skyline. The view can be seen at its best if you cross the bridge at sunrise or sunset. You can get back to Manhattan by taking the subway, routes 2 or 3, from Clark Street Station. The entrance is to the east of City Hall in Park Row/Centre Street.
Subway: Brooklyn Bridge / City Hall, 4, 5, 6

Chelsea Piers (108/C3)
A part of the dilapidated pier on the Hudson River has been reborn as the *Chelsea Piers Sports & Entertainment Complex.* Aside from photographic and film studios, there are several cafés and good restaurants, in-line skating rinks *(Pier 62),* two ice skating rinks *(Pier 61),* a gigantic fitness club *(Pier 60,* daily membership $31) and a four-storey *driving range* for golfers.
Hudson River and 23rd Street, Tel: 336-6666, Subway: 23rd Street, C, E, then bus M 23

The Cloisters (O)
The Cloisters complex in the middle of Fort Tryon Park was built between 1934 and 1938 from the remains of four cloisters brought over from France and Spain. The combination of Gothic and Romanesque styles together with the surrounding landscaped gardens exemplify the passion Americans had for European architectural styles. The Cloisters was a gift to the city from John D. Rockefeller, Jr, and today houses the Metropolitan Museum's collection of medieval art. There is a lovely view from here of the George Washington Bridge and the steep, tree-lined banks of the Hudson River on the New Jersey side. *Tues-Sun, 9.30-16.45; admission: voluntary donations (suggested amount: $8); Fort Tryon Park; Tel: 923-3700; Subway: 190th Street, A; Bus: 4, Cloisters-Fort Tryon Park (bus stop on Madison Avenue between 32nd and 110th Street)*

Columbus Circle (105/E3)
Buffeted by loud traffic on all sides, this statue stands at the crossroads of Broadway, Central Park South, Central Park West and Eighth Avenue. It was erected in 1892 to celebrate the 400th anniversary of the discovery of America by Christopher Columbus. Central Park is within comfortable walking distance. *Subway: 59th Street, 1, 9, A, B, C, D*

Grand Central Station (106/A6)
★ To make way for the great New York station, built in 1913, 2.5 million square metres of earth were removed to northern Manhattan, 25 km (16 mi) of iron tracks were laid and 18,000 tonnes of steel were used in its

construction. The concourse is larger than the nave of Notre Dame in Paris. The façade is decorated in the Beaux-Arts style and above the windows, some of which stretch up to 25 m (83 ft), the ceiling is painted with a winter sky filled with thousands of stars. It's been a while now since long-distance trains stopped running from this station, but commuter trains from Westchester County and Connecticut still stop here. The station is currently being renovated to recapture the splendour of bygone days. It boasts a bar, a café, a fish restaurant and live music shows. Sightseeing tour by the Municipal Art Society. *Wed 12.30; Tel: 935-3960; Suggested contribution: $5; East 42nd Street, between Vanderbilt* *and Lexington Avenue; Subway: Grand Central, 4, 5, 6 and 7*

Rockefeller Center (105/F5)

★ Oil magnate and philanthropist, John D. Rockefeller, Jr, originally planned to use the 25-acre area between 48th Street and 51st Street, and Fifth and Sixth Avenue, in the centre of Manhattan, as the site for the Metropolitan Opera. The Wall Street Crash of 1929 put a stop to these plans and so instead, during the 1930s, Rockefeller demolished 228 houses to make way for his 'city within the city'. This high-rise complex constitutes 14 sandstone skyscrapers, including the 70-storey GE Building, squares, gardens, Radio City Music Hall, Christie's and numerous shops

MARCO POLO SELECTION: SIGHTSEEING

and underground shopping streets. At the heart of the Rockefeller Center lies the Ice Rink bordered by the tables of the American Festival Café (except in the summer). Every year at the beginning of December, the lights are ceremoniously lit on the tallest Christmas tree in New York – a 25 m (82 ft) high fir tree from Maine.

The entrance to the small Rockefeller Center Museum is in the concourse where maps, architectural models and old photos are displayed. You can get maps of the Rockefeller Center free of charge in the lobby.
30 Rockefeller Plaza, between 49th and 50th Street; Subway: 47th-50th Street, B, D, F, Q

St John the Divine (101/D1)
Though still unfinished, this is, or will be, the biggest cathedral in the world, covering a greater area than Chartres and Notre Dame put together. As with many buildings in New York, it was built in a somewhat indiscriminate mixture of styles. Construction began in 1892 with predominantly Byzantine and Romanesque influences, and was then continued in 1911 by architects influenced mainly by Gothic styles. It will not be completed until the next century, but it's well worth a visit. Poetry readings, plays and concerts are held here in the evenings. *Amsterdam Avenue/112th Street; Tel: 316-7540; Subway: 110th Street, 1, 9*

St. Patrick's Cathedral (106/A4)
Situated between the Rockefeller Center, the Olympic Tower and Saks Fifth Avenue, this neo-Gothic stone and marble cathe-dral was built in 1879 on what is now the most expensive land in New York. Dedicated to the patron saint of Ireland, it is the seat of the Archbishop of New York and is the eleventh largest church in the world, accommodating a congregation of 2500. It is open all day to anyone wishing to escape the clamour of Fifth Avenue. *5th Avenue/50th Street; Subway: 47th-50th Street, B, D, F, Q*

Statue of Liberty (O)
'Miss Liberty' is 46 m (152 ft) high, with a 47 m pedestal and weighs 225 tonnes. Erected in 1886 by the French sculptor Frédéric-Auguste Bartholdi to-gether with Gustave Eiffel, the statue stands as a symbol of liber-ty dedicated to millions of immi-grants who flocked to the USA. A lift takes you up 10 storeys to the top of the pedestal. The next 12 storeys have to be climbed on foot. The view from the crown is onto Manhattan, Brooklyn and New Jersey. *Lifts are every 30 min-utes, 9.30-16.00, from the Office of the Circle Line in Castle Clinton, Battery Park; admission: $7; Liberty Island; Tel: 269-5755; Subway: South Ferry, 1, 9*

Trinity Church (114/B5)
This Episcopal church on Wall Street has actually been built three times. The original build-ing, erected in 1698 and financed by taxes collected from the local Anglican community, was made of wood and burnt down in the Great Fire of 1776. The church built to replace it was demol-ished in 1839 after its roof col-lapsed, when the present struc-ture was erected. There is a small cemetery adjacent to the church, where prominent New Yorkers

Relaxing in the Winter Garden of the World Financial Center

are buried. *Broadway (Wall Street); Subway: Rector Street, 1, 9, R*

Waldorf-Astoria (106/B5)

This luxury 1930s hotel spans a whole block and is resplendent in all its *art deco* glory. There used to be a special platform for wealthy guests travelling to this 2000-room hotel by train, but the nearest you can get on the train now is Grand Central Station. The hotel ballrooms still bear traces of the glamour, splendour and opulence of its heyday. *301 Park Avenue, between 49th and 50th Street; Tel: 355-3000; Subway: 51st Street, E, F, 6*

World Financial Center (114/A4)

★ The World Financial Center lies within Battery Park City on the southern tip of Manhattan. It was designed by Alexander Cooper, with the help of a number of other New York architects, and built on reclaimed land. The complex includes offices (mostly of financial companies), shops and apartments, a marina and, at its heart, the magnificent steel and glass atrium – the Winter Garden. The entrance to this huge public space is on the North Bridge and a pedestrian overpass runs between Vesey Street and the World Trade Center. In the Winter Garden you can listen to concerts or just sit and read among the palm trees and marble splendour. Alternatively, you can visit some of the 40-odd shops and restaurants in the Plaza. *West Street, between Vesey and Liberty Street; Subway: Cortlandt Street/ World Trade Center, 1, 9*

CULTURE

Apollo Theater (O)

An excellent reason for taking a trip to Harlem would be to visit this theatre, built in 1914. Every

17

Wednesday evening, young black performers come and put their talent to the test.

253 West 125th Street, between Adam Clayton Powell Jr and Frederick Douglas Boulevard; Tel: 749-5838; Subway: 125th Street, 1, 9

Carnegie Hall (105/E4)

The concert hall first opened in 1891 when Tchaikovsky himself conducted the inaugural concert before a packed house (2760 seats). It is still as prestigious a venue for world-class musicians and orchestras today. To celebrate its centenary, $50 million was spent on renovation. If you want a peek behind the scenes, backstage tours of the Hall are held at regular intervals.

Mon, Tues, Thurs, Fri 11.30, 14.00 and 15.00; admission: $6; 57th Street/7th Avenue; Tel: 247-7800; Subway: 57th Street, N, R

Columbia University (101/D1)

⚲ The campus buildings of New York's most prestigious university were designed in the Beaux-Arts and Renaissance style by architects McKim, Mead & White. Take a short walk through the grounds and you will be rubbing shoulders with the next generation of top academics.

Between Broadway/Morningside Drive and 114th/120th Street; Subway: 116th Street, 1, 9

Lincoln Center (105/D2–3)

This vast complex is the cultural nerve-centre of New York. It covers eight blocks and can seat up to 15, 000 spectators at a time in its seven concert halls and theatres. The Plaza lies at the heart of the Lincoln Center and, in summer, a variety of open air plays and per-

formances are held here. Entrance to any of the theatre lobbies is free. There is a huge Chagall mural in the Metropolitan Opera House (back stage tour $8, *Tel: 769-7020)* and the Center's own restaurant, *Panevino (Tel: 874-7000),* is in the Avery Fisher Hall. *Broadway/ 62nd Street; Tel: 875-5000; Subway: 66th Street, 1, 9*

New York Public Library (105/F6)

This grand Beaux-Arts building on Fifth Avenue, with its neo-classical façade flanked by stone lions, was first opened in 1911. Not only avid readers pass through the great bronze doors. Many people visit the library just to admire the wood-panelled lobby and the vast reading room (which is in the process of being equipped with Internet access) filled with long wooden reading tables, or to take in one of the various exhibitions held there. The library's collection, comprising nine million books and 22 million manuscripts, includes Thomas Jefferson's handwritten copy of the Declaration of Independence, a Gutenberg bible and documents written by Galileo. *Mon, Thurs, Fri, Sat 10.00-18.00, Tues/Wed 11.00-19.30; guided tours: Tel: 930-0501; 5th Avenue between 40th and 42nd Streets; Tel: 930-0800; Subway: 42nd Street, B, D, F, Q*

Radio City Music Hall (105/F5)

This splendid *art deco* concert hall in the Rockefeller Center can hold up to 6000 visitors. When it opened in 1932, it was the largest in the world, with sunken stages and the latest technical fittings and equipment. Rock concerts are held here as well as film previews shown on a huge screen, not forgetting the popular Christmas and Easter shows featuring the Rockettes, the resident high-kicking dance troupe. *Visiting hours: Mon-Sat 10.00-17.00, Sun 11.00-17.00; admission: $13.75; Tel: 632-4041; 1260 Avenue of the Americas, between 50th and 51st Street; Tel: 247-4777 (tickets); Subway: 47th-50th Street, B, D*

DISTRICTS

Borough Park   (O)
This Jewish enclave in Brooklyn is the haven and centre for the largest number of orthodox Jews outside Israel. Shops and restaurants close for the Sabbath by Friday afternoon. There are around 200 synagogues and 50 Talmudic schools in the district. The Purim festival in spring draws 25,000 visitors to the area along 13th Avenue.

Brooklyn Heights   (115/E–F5–6)
⚓ Lying right by Brooklyn Bridge, this is one of the most beautiful residential areas in Brooklyn. It boasts a high concentration of well-preserved brownstones. These magnificent four- or five-storey red-brick houses used to accommodate just one family per building and many of them are now classified as historical monuments (the brownstones in Brooklyn Heights have been listed buildings since 1965). Pierrepont Street leads to the Brooklyn Heights Promenade where you will be captivated by the stunning view of Manhattan. Montague Street is lined with shops and restaurants. *Subway: Clark Street, 2, 3*

Chelsea   (109/D–E2–3)
⚴ This peaceful residential area between Seventh Avenue and the Hudson River, and 14th and 29th Street, has always been a favourite with writers, actors and painters. Many have been guests at the Chelsea Hotel (222 West 23rd Street), where each room has its own decorative style. Illustrious guests have included Mark Twain, Arthur Miller and Tennessee Williams. You can wander in and look around the lobby without having to book a room. Today Chelsea is lined with new galleries, many bars and boutiques and there are plenty of restaurants on Eighth Avenue between 14th and 23rd Street that attract a predominantly young crowd. *Subway: 23rd Street, C, E*

Chinatown   (115/C2–3)
❧ Almost half of the 300,000 Chinese people living in New York are concentrated in Chinatown. It is a colourful and bustling world, where the streets are a constant buzz of activity. English is far from being the most common language here, and wherever you look you will see Chinese characters. There are numerous restaurants in and around Mott, Bayard and Pell Streets, where prices are low by comparison to the rest of New York. Many restaurants in Chinatown do not have a 'liquor license'. You can bring your own beer or wine, but will have to pay a small corkage fee ($3). *Subway: Canal Street, 6, J, R*

East Village   (110/B–C5–6)
The last few years have witnessed an influx of artists to this Jewish-Polish-Russian quarter, a former low-rent district that lies between the Bowery and Avenue A, and 1st and 12th Street. Now that the rents are inevitably rising, strug-

Central Park: almost twice the size of Monaco

gling artists are being forced to seek new pastures. Nevertheless, it is still a lively place. There is a wide variety of ethnic restaurants offering reasonably priced meals. The following are recommended: *Khyber Pass (34 St. Mark's Place,* Afghan food) and *Boca Chica (13 1st Avenue,* South American food). *Subway: Astor Place, 6*

Flatiron District (110/A3–4)

Just 10 years ago, the area between 14th and 23rd Street and Union Square and Fifth Avenue was still a real no-man's land. Now you can find designer boutiques, photographers' studios, restaurants and cafés throughout the district named after the triangular Renaissance Palazzo-style skyscraper, built in 1902 (where Broadway crosses Fifth Avenue). It is called the Flatiron Building because its shape resembles an iron with no handle.
Subway: 14th Street/Union Square, 4, 5, 6, L, R

Greenwich Village (109/E–F5–6)

Right up until the 1960s, Greenwich Village was frequented by artists, writers and lecturers from New York University. Today, it is an expensive residential area free of skyscrapers. Some of the houses have wonderful stoops leading up to the front door, a rare feature in modern New York. Many of the brownstones and townhouses here date back to the beginning of the 19th century, when the Village was situated towards the north of the city. In this area, the narrow streets have names instead of numbers. *Subway: Christopher Street, 1, 9*

Harlem (101/E–F1)

In 1658, Dutch settlers named the area in which they had settled 'Nieuw Haarlem'. Later, black slaves built a road from here to New York (which then covered just the southern tip of Manhattan) called Broadway. Many of these slaves ended up staying there. In the 1920s and 1930s, Harlem became a nucleus of black creativity. It was chic to listen to jazz musicians such as Duke Ellington and Count Basie at the Sugar Cane or Cotton Club *(today, Gospel Brunch, Sat, Sun, Tel: 663-7980).* Since the 1960s, however, it is reputed to be one of the most dangerous areas in New York for whites to visit. Probably the best way to see the district with its beautiful but decayed turn-of-the-century buildings is with friends who know their way around Harlem or with an organized tour. *Harlem Spirituals, Tel: 757-0425, or Harlem Your Way!, Tel: 690-1687*

Little Italy (114/C1–2)

Italian immigrants have been settling here since the beginning of the 20th century, though today they don't have an easy time of it: there is a steady stream of immigrants from Hong Kong flowing over the old Chinatown border, Canal Street. Yuppies are moving into the expensive apartments in the area and tourists jostle along its streets. Yet, despite all this, you can still observe the way of life and comings and goings of the mamas, papas and their bambini. Take it all in from one of the many restaurant tables that spill out onto the pavement. A great way to spend a summer's day. *Subway: Grand Street, B, D, Q*

SoHo (114/B1–2)

The name of this district is derived from its location: SoHo stands for South of Houston Street. The area between Broadway and Avenue of the Americas was discovered by artists at the beginning of the 1970s when the deserted factory spaces were transformed into flats (known as lofts) and studios. Galleries and boutiques followed suit. SoHo has since become known as one of the best shopping areas in New York. The cast-iron façades that feature on many of the buildings, in Greene Street for example, are an impressive sight. *Subway: Prince Street, R*

Theater District (105/E5–6)

During the day, this area north of Times Square comes to life *(for example, the Disney Store, 42nd Street/Seventh Avenue).* After 7 pm, the neon lights start flashing and people pack the theatres. After the shows, crowds pour into Restaurant Row (46th Street between Eighth and Ninth Avenue). Times Square is a huge renovation project. During the 1920s there were around 50 small theatres in this area. Today, these beautiful but less profitable venues are disappearing fast and being replaced with cinemas, hotels and restaurants. The largest restaurants are *Broadway Grill (1605 Broadway)* and the *All-Star Café (1540 Broadway).* Once a year, Times Square, with its famous newswire, is the focal point of the city: on 31 December, approximately 100,000 New Yorkers gather here to ring in the New Year. *Subway: 42nd Street/Times Square, 1, 2, 3, 7, 9, N, R*

TriBeCa (114/A–B2–3)

Like SoHo, the name of this district derives from its location: triangle below canal. It used to be the city's market area, formerly known as Washington Market. When the market stopped trading, creative (and far-sighted)

New Yorkers moved into the huge warehouses and transformed them into lofts. A number of celebrities have invested in TriBeCa, increasing its value. Among them are Oscar-winning actor Robert de Niro (with his TriBeCa Film Group on Greenwich Street), dramatist Edward Albee and director Robert Wilson. Many of the city's newest restaurants open up here, the best of which are located in and around Duane Street. *Subway: Franklin Street, 1, 9*

Upper East Side (106/A–C1–3)

The Upper East Side stretches from Central Park to East River and from 59th to 79th Street. Ever since the end of the 19th century, it has been regarded as one of the city's smartest and most elegant districts, highly sought after by those who can afford it. Small, chic boutiques and numerous restaurants lure New Yorkers into the area from all over the city. Among its other attractions, the Upper East Side boasts countless museums, galleries and some very smart hotels.

Upper West Side (105/D1–2)

This newly gentrified area, lying between 65th and 85th Streets, first became a popular residential district for successful and wealthy young people in the early 1980s. It is centred around Columbus Avenue, where countless boutiques have since appeared, and Amsterdam Avenue, where a crop of lively restaurants has sprung up, while the sector of Broadway that cuts through it is lined with banks and gourmet shops. Focal points of cultural interest in this district are the Lincoln Center, with the Met-

ropolitan Opera, and the American Museum of Natural History.

Wall Street (114/B5)

This surprisingly short street is the stock-dealing hub of the world. It lies within the Financial District and is home to many national and international banks. The entrance to New York Stock Exchange on Broad Street is just a stone's throw away. An incredible 250 million shares are dealt there every day. Young men and women in sombre suits (and trainers!), clutching briefcases, can be seen rushing to and from their offices. The street comes to life around 12.30 when the Wall Street yuppies swarm outside for a bite to eat. A quick sandwich is usually all they have time for. *Subway: Wall Street, 2, 3, 4, 5*

MARKETS

Fulton Fish Market (114/C4)

★ If you can haul yourself out of bed early enough, this market is well worth the effort. Between 04.00 and 08.00 every day, around 75,000 wholesalers sell about 350,000 pounds of fish. There are over 500 different varieties on offer. Especially impressive are the giant tuna fish which are cut into steaks for the purchasing fishmongers. After visiting the market, you can watch the sunrise over the East River while sipping a coffee at the bar on the corner – though it may taste a little fishy! There are guided tours from April to October on the first and third Thursdays of the month ($10). *South Street/Fulton Street; Tel: 748-8590 (tours); Subway: Fulton Street, 2, 3, 4, 5, J*

Gansevoort Market (109/E4)
This is New York's main meat market where meat is sold wholesale between 5 and 8 am. Have a wander round (again, it'll have to be early) and finish off your visit with a *boudin* (sausage) at Florent's bistro. *Gansevoort/Greenwich Street; Subway: 14th Street, A, C, E*

PARKS & GARDENS

Bronx Zoo (O)
There are over 650 different species housed here (4200 animals in total), many of which are accommodated in areas specially created to resemble their natural habitat. A shuttle train service operates through a section of the zoo. The New York Botanical Garden and the Enid Haupt Conservatory, home to tropical and desert flora, are just next door.
10.00-17.00; admission: $6.75; Bronx Park; Tel: 367-1010; Bus: Liberty Lines ($4) from Madison Ave.

Brooklyn Botanic Garden (O)
This garden was designed in 1910 by New York's celebrated landscape architect Frederick Law Olmsted. It contains various theme gardens, including three Japanese meditation gardens, a Shakespeare garden, a rose garden and America's largest Bonsai collection, with 900 different species. *Garden and conservatory: April-September. Tues-Fri 08.00-18.00 (winter 16.30), Sat/Sun 10.00-18.00; admission: $3, free on Tues; 1000 Washington Avenue, Brooklyn; Tel: 622-4433; Subway: Eastern Parkway, 2, 3*

Central Park (105/E-F1-3)
★ It took two decades of design and planning, under the direction of Frederick Law Olmsted, before Central Park was finally opened in 1873. With its winding drives, large meadows, ponds, monuments and statues, the park, which stretches from 59th to 110th Street, covers over 850 acres – roughly twice the size of Monaco! New Yorkers frequent the park from dawn until dusk: they jog around the reservoir (upper 90th Street), row on the lake ($10 an hour), hire bicycles *(The Boathouse, near East 72nd Street; Tel: 861-4137; $8/hr)*, skate in winter, roller-blade *(Blades 120 West 72nd Street; Tel: 787-3911,*

New York movies
A small grating on Lexington Avenue marks the spot where Marilyn Monroe's white dress billowed up in the gust of air stirred by a passing subway train. It was this image from *The Seven Year Itch* that immortalized Monroe. The classic comedy is just one among countless films set in New York that have gone down in movie history: *King Kong, The Godfather, Taxi Driver* and *French Connection* to name but a few – not forgetting, of course, the many Woody Allen films shot in his beloved city. Manhattan's most recent cinematic attraction is the vast and technologically superb IMAX film palace where excellent entertainment is guaranteed. Broadway (corner of 68th Street).

$16/hr) or play minigolf in the summer *(Wollman Memorial Rink; Tel: 396-1010; $4 plus skate hire)*, visit Central Park Zoo, meet in the Boathouse Café or lie in the sun. Open-air concerts are held here in the summertime and are free of charge. But the area should definitely be avoided after dark! *Subway: 59th Street, 1, 9, A, B, C, D and many other stations along the Park borders.*

Coney Island (O)
This is the only beach in the world that can be reached by subway. It boasts a pleasure park and the legendary boardwalk which has been classified as a historic monument. Don't miss the hot dogs at Nathan's. On weekends, if the weather's good, half a million people will flock here. Just next door is the New York Aquarium featuring an enormous shark pool.
Surf Avenue, Brooklyn; Subway: Coney Island, B, D, F, N

Greenwood (O)
This vast Brooklyn cemetery, with its meandering paths, rolling hills, ponds and lakes, covers 500 acres and is one of the largest cemeteries in the world. It was designed in the mid-19th century and based on the Père Lachaise cemetery in Paris. You can get an excellent view of the Manhattan skyline from here, and if you wander around Greenwood, you'll come across the impressive memorial stones of many a great entrepreneur who is buried here, including the jeweller Louis Comfort Tiffany, pencil manufacturer Eberhard Faber, toothpaste magnate Wil-

liam Colgate and piano-maker Henry Steinway.
Subway: 25th Street, N, R

Washington Square (110/A5)
★ ‡ This animated square in the heart of Greenwich Village was once a cemetery. It is one of the few green spaces in downtown New York and today it is very much alive with street musicians, children, joggers, strollers and students from the nearby New York University. Within it stands the Washington Arch, erected to commemorate the centenary of the first U.S. President coming to power.
Subway: West 4th Street, A, B, C, D, E, F, Q

POLITICS & HISTORY

Bartow Pell Mansion (O)
This former 18th-century manor house was renovated in 1842 in the Greek Revival style. It lies within a 200-acre park and houses a large collection of original Empire furniture.
Wed, Sat and Sun 12.00-16.00; admission: $2.50; Shore Road North, Pelham Bay Park; Tel: 885-1461; Subway: Pelham Bay Park, 6

Bowne House (O)
This Quaker house was built in 1661 by John Bowne, who was arrested for his religious beliefs by the tyrannical governor Peter Stuyvesant. Over nine generations of the Bowne family lived in this house, which has been preserved as an important showpiece of early American history.
Tues, Sat and Sun 14.30-16.30; admission: $2; 37-01 Bowne Street, Flushing, Queens; Tel: (718) 359-0528; Subway: Main Street, 7

City Hall (114/B3)

When it was first built in 1812, the southern façade of City Hall, the mayor's official seat of government, was clad in snow-white marble while the northern façade was merely brick-covered, left unadorned because the city elders had not expected the city to develop further northwards. The court buildings are situated in the near vicinity and on the east side of Centre Street is the Municipal Building, where New Yorkers – and tourists – can purchase a marriage licence for just $30.

Between Broadway and Park Row; Tel: 669-2400; Subway: City Hall, R

Ellis Island (O)

About 12 million immigrants passed through the gates of Ellis Island between 1892 and 1954. The transit camp, comprising 33 buildings in all, served as a control centre where immigrants were checked, registered and examined, before being permitted

Fifth Avenue: along stretch of luxury, opulence and wealth

entrance to their new country. Built on the small island in New York Bay not far from the Statue of Liberty, the site was renovated in 1990 using $156 million of private funds and is now open to the public. Only the main building has been restored – the fate of the remaining buildings, including the former hospital, remains uncertain. *Daily 10.00-15.30, summer: 9.30–16, ferry every half hour; $7 (Statue of Liberty Line); Departure: Battery Park; Subway: South Ferry, 1, 9*

Fraunces Tavern   (114/B6)
The main house, originally built in 1719, is where Commander of the American Forces George Washington made his farewell speech to his officers. This house and the five 19th-century brick buildings surrounding it have all been accurately restored and furnished. The restaurant has been running since 1763. It has a large fireplace and serves traditional American dishes, such as Yankee Roast. *Restaurant: Mon-Fri 7.00-10.00; 11.30-16.00, 17.00-21.30,Tel: 269-0144; Museum: Mon-Fri 10.00-16.45, Sat 12.00-16.00; admission $2.50; 54 Pearl Street/Broad Street; Tel: 425-1778; Subway: Whitehall Street, LR4,5*

Morris-Jumel Mansion   (O)
This pre-Revolutionary mansion located in Washington Heights, is named after George Washington, who used to keep watch from this natural vantage point during the War of Independence, as it lent an excellent view over the Hudson and East rivers. The Palladian-style mansion, now a museum, was once the temporary army headquarters. Beyond it lies Sylvan Terrace, a row of wooden houses dating back to 1882. *Wed-Sun 10.00-16.00; admission $3; West 160th Street/Edgecombe Avenue; Tel: 923-8008; Subway: 163rd Street 1B, at the Weekend C*

New York Stock Exchange   (114/B5)
Right in the heart of the frenetic Financial District stands the magnificent neo-classical building that houses the New York Stock Exchange. From the Public Viewing Gallery you can watch the activity on the Trading Floor below, where frantically gesticulating brokers buy and sell shares. *Mon-Fri 09.15-16.00; taped commentaries; admission free of charge but limited number of tickets available; 20 Broad Street; Tel: 656-5167; Subway: Whitehall Street, R, and Wall Street, 2, 3, 4, 5*

Old Merchant's House   (110/B6)
Built in 1832, this house first belonged to a wealthy iron merchant and is the only 19th-century building in New York with all its original fixtures and fittings intact. *Sun-Thurs 13.00-16.00; admission $3; 29 East 4th Street, between Lafayette Street and the Bowery; Tel: 777-1089; Subway: Astor Place, 6*

United Nations   (106/C5)
A steel and glass complex of skyscrapers, designed by an international board of architects (including Le Corbusier), which has been the United Nations headquarters since the 1950s, is the central office for UN organizations such as UNESCO. A guided tour will lead you through the entrance hall where works of art from around the world are exhibited, and to the room in which

the General Assembly holds its annual meeting. *Every 15 mins between 09.15 and 16.45; United Nations Plaza, 1st Avenue/45th Street; Tel: 963-7539; Subway: 51st Street, 6*

SKYLINE

Staten Island Ferry (114/B6)
★ ᚈ᚜ One of the cheapest pleasures that New York has to offer also provides the most spectacular view of Manhattan's skyline; the ferry ride will take you to Staten Island and back, past the Lady Liberty and Ellis Island, for free.
South Street/State Street, in the day-time every 30 mins, and from 23.00-06.00 every hour; Subway: South Ferry, 1, 9 (first five carriages only at the front of the train)
Other excellent vantage points for a view of the skyline:
ᚈ᚜ observation deck on the 107th floor of the *World Trade Center* and restaurants
ᚈ᚜ observatories on the 86th and 102nd floors of the Empire State Building *(summer until 24.00)*
ᚈ᚜ terrace of the *River Café* in Brooklyn
ᚈ᚜ the rooftop bar of the *Peninsula Hotel*
ᚈ᚜ the *Rainbow Room* bar in the Rockefeller Center (GE Building), especially on the 4th of July
ᚈ᚜ the rooftop *Sculpture Garden* of the Metropolitan Museum
ᚈ᚜ the meadows of *Central Park*

SKYSCRAPERS

Chrysler Building (106/B6)
This wonderful *art deco* building, completed in 1930, is a favourite with New Yorkers. Even though

The magnificent spire of the Chrysler Building is a real work of art

there's no access to the top, it's still well worth a visit just to see the lavishly decorated lobby with its ornate wooden elevator doors, beautiful marble floor and painted ceiling. The sky-scraper was designed by the architect William van Alen who was commissioned by the Chrysler automobile corpora-tion. He based the design,which was popular at the time, on a typical early 1930s Chrysler automobile, crowned with a spire whose lines reflect those of a radiator grill with its radiator caps. *405 Lexington Av-enue, between 42nd and 43rd Street; Sub-way: Grand Central, 4, 5, 6, 7*

Citicorp Center (106/B4)
This white 59-storey skyscraper has a distinctive angled roof,

which was originally designed to operate as a solar collector, but it never functioned and is now used only as a vent for the air-conditioning system. Its silhouette stands out on the Manhattan skyline and when lit up at night it can be seen for miles. The lower storeys are host to shops and restaurants, public lavatories (a rarity in New York) and a seating area where you can sit and relax.
Lexington/3rd Avenue and 53rd/54th Street; Subway: 51st Street, 6

Empire State Building (110/A1)
★ ◁⁄▷ This 407 m (1340 ft) high, 102-storey building is one of the classic symbols of New York. At night, the top 30 floors can be lit up in a variety of colours. On the 4th of July they are floodlit in red, white and blue. The building opened in 1931 and took only 18 months to build. At the ticket office in the basement (entrance on 34th Street) make sure you don't miss the marble and bronze-lined lobby. There are two observation decks: the round glass observatory on the 86th floor and the observatory on the 102nd floor. On a clear day, you can see for a distance of 80 km (50 mi).
Daily 9.30-24.00; admission: $6; ticket including Skyride action cinema: $14; 350 5th Avenue/34th Street; Subway: 34th Street, B, D, F, N, Q, R

590 Madison (106/A4)
The lobby of this 43-storey tower (formerly *IBM building*) is an excellent place to sit down and relax among the bamboo trees and tropical plants, with coffee and croissants from the café.
Tues-Fri 11.00-18.00, Sat 10.00-17.00; admission free; 590 Madison Avenue between 56th and 57th Street; Subway: 59th Street, 4, 5, 6

Seagram Building (106/A4)
This bronze and glass building – weathered to a metallic black – was built in 1958 and is the only Mies van der Rohe building in New York. It is typical of the International Style so characteristic of America at that time. The interior of the in-house restaurant, the *Four Seasons*, is very much in keeping with the period and is classified as a historical landmark. To the south of the building, on both sides of Park Avenue, is a row of skyscrapers

The Empire State Building — over sixty years old and still one of the most popular landmarks in New York City

erected in the 1950s, which have long since been overshadowed by much taller buildings: *Lever House (390 Park Avenue, between 53rd and 54th Street)* and the *Met-Life (formerly PanAm) Building* (on the corner of 45th Street and Park Avenue) which, according to many architects, is Manhattan's ugliest skyscraper, looming over Grand Central Station. The MetLife building was designed by Mies van der Rohe's Bauhaus colleague Walter Gropius, together with Emery Roth and Sons and Pietro Belluschi.
375 Park Avenue, between 52nd and 53rd Street; Subway: 51st Street, 6

Sony Building (106/A4)

♱ This rose granite building was designed by Philip Johnson, the doyen of New York architects. It was originally the headquarters of the telephone corporation AT&T, but has since been taken over by the Japanese electronics corporation Sony, thus making a statement in New York The post-modernist feature of a semicircular incision in the centre of the sloping roof has been nicknamed 'Chippendale' after the style of the furniture-maker. The lobby is open to the public. It is a paradise for those who love electronic gadgets: Sony walkmans, telephones, televisions, etc. are all sold here. The history of technological communication is told in the *Sony Wonderlab, (Tues-Sat 10.00-18.00, Sun 12.00-18.00* Tel 833-8100), and you can even hire computers and videos and rent recording studios. *550 Madison Avenue, between 55th and 56th Street; Subway: 5th Avenue, N, R*

Trump Tower (106/A4)

A monument to the New York real estate speculator Donald Trump, which he himself commissioned. Although his empire has since begun to crumble, the 68-storey residential tower block is still as elegant as ever, with its opulent pink marble and bronze atrium complete with waterfall, that encompasses five storeys and houses the most exclusive shops. If you fancy a break, why not stop off at the self-service café in the basement.
725 5th Avenue, between 56th and 57th Street; Subway: 5th Avenue, N, R

World Trade Center (114/A–B4)

⬆ There are 50,000 employees working in the 110-storey twin towers, and a further 75,000 people visit the centre each day to see the view from New York's highest buildings (450 m/1480 ft). On a clear day, visibility reaches up to 80 km (50 mi) and the view is especially spectacular at sunset. There is a glass observation deck on the southern tower as well as an outside roof deck, which is closed if it is at all windy. The elevator trip to the 107th floor is 58 seconds (*admission: $10; daily 09.30-21.30, in summer until 23.30, Tel: 323-2340*).

The bomb that went off in the underground car park in the spring of 1993 destroyed five stor-eys in the basement area. Smoke and water caused considerable damage to the rest of the building, but all traces of the destruction have since been eliminated.

Not to be missed are the restaurants *Windows on the World* and *Cellar in the Sky (Tel: 524-7011; both Category 1)* and the *Greatest Bar on Earth* on the 107th floor.

From there, the greatest city on earth lies at your feet! *Subway: World Trade Center, 1, 9, C, E, N, R*

STREETS & AVENUES

Avenue of the Americas   (105/F4–5)
During the second construction phase of the Rockefeller Center in the 1950s, a row of skyscrapers was built along the Avenue of the Americas (Sixth Avenue) which became known as the 'tomb-stones' because of the way they were laid out. The following buildings can be found to the north of 47th Street, on the west side of the Avenue, each one spanning an entire block: the Celanese Building, the McGraw-Hill Building, the Exxon Building, the Time Life Building and, between 51st and 52nd Streets, the Equitable Center. *Lobby opening hours: 08.00-18.00; Subway: 47th-50th Street, B, D, F, Q*

Broadway   (101/D1–114/B5)
The most famous street in New York is also the longest and the only diagonal street on the grid. It stretches northwards from Manhattan's southern tip for almost 21 km (13 mi) and goes from the East Side through Midtown, across to Upper West Side and on up to Harlem. It is multi-faceted, boasting new shops in the old

soho district, encompassing the Theater District and neon-lit Times Square and passing through the ghetto areas where it witness to a harsher reality.

Canal Street   (114/A–C2)
Canal Street separates the West Village and SoHo from TriBeCa and runs between Little Italy and Chinatown. For the best overall view of the area, try walking on a Saturday from Sixth Avenue eastwards towards Manhattan Bridge. There is nothing that can't be bought on Canal Street (in the shops or on the street). In Chinatown you'll find excellent fish and vegetable stores – the main reason why uptowners make the journey downtown. *Subway: Canal Street, A, C, E*

Central Park West   (105/E1–3)
In 1884, building proprietors had to come up with something really special in order to entice tenants away from Fifth Avenue to the opposite side of Central Park, which at that time was far from fashionable. Rooms were therefore designed to be extraordinarily large and staff were provided to service the blocks. This is how *The Dakota* came into being on the north side of 72nd Street (the building in which John Lennon lived and in front of which he

30

was shot in 1980). Other notable buildings are the *Beresford (81st Street)*, the *San Remo (74/75th Street)* and the *Hotel Des Artistes (1 West 67th Street)*.

Take a breather on a bench in *Strawberry Fields*, the section of Central Park opposite The Dakota that has been restored and maintained by the instigation and funding of John Lennon's widow, Yoko Ono. Or visit the garden of the *Tavern on the Green*, one of the two restaurants in the Park.
Subway: 72nd Street, B, C

Christopher Street   (109/E5)
New York's gay population is centred around the heart of Greenwich Village. In Christopher and Gay Streets, there are many pubs and shops catering exclusively for gays.
Subway: Christopher Street, 1, 9

Diamond District   (105/F5)
In 47th Street, between Fifth and Sixth Avenues, lie the offices and shops of diamond merchants, who are mostly orthodox Jews dressed entirely in black This is the centre of New York's jewellery industry where millions of dollars change hands every day. *Subway: 47th-50th Street, B, D, F, Q*

Fifth Avenue   (106/A1–6)
★ Fifth Avenue, which starts at Washington Square, serves a very important function in Manhattan's street network as it marks the dividing line between West and East. It is Manhattan's showpiece street where New York shows off to its best advantage its glamorous shops (like Tiffany's and Bergdorf Goodman), its splendid museums (Metropolitan, Guggenheim), its

impressive architecture (the Rockefeller Center) and sheer grandeur (the Empire State Building). It is also host to some of New York's largest and most spectacular parades (e.g. the St. Patrick's Day parade).

Madison Avenue   (106/A1–6)
Even though the head offices of America's main advertising agencies now tend to be located in other cities, the name of Madison Avenue is still synonymous with the elite of the advertising industry. This glamorous avenue between 44th Street and 86th Street is also lined with salons of most of the top European couturiers and American fashion houses. Those who rely on public transport and do not necessarily want to use a taxi, will find the Avenue has an added bonus, because it is the only one in New York with two special bus lanes. This guarantees speedy progress to where-ever one wishes to be in this busy street, even in the rush hour.

St. Mark's Place   (110/B–C5)
★ This street (8th Street) lies at the heart of the Polish and Ukrainian district and really should not be missed if one's fancies are shops, selling second-hand clothes and other bric-a-brac treasures, restaurants and cafés.This area is home to many artists, as the price of studios are still within their means. Why not stop for a breather at the *Ukrainian (140 2nd Avenue)*, which serves Ukrainian specialities, *Veselka (144 2nd Avenue)* or at *Teresa's (103 1st Avenue)*, where you can savour Polish-Jewish specialities such as cheese blintzes (pancakes with sour cream). *Subway: 1st Avenue , L*

An art lover's Mecca

New York boasts some of the world's greatest collections, from prehistoric to contemporary art

For a long time, American museums were regarded as the poor relations to their great ancestors across the Atlantic, such as the Louvre in Paris and the National Gallery in London. Europe, it seemed, held the monopoly on culture, heritage and tradition. During the last 100 years or so, however, a fascinating cultural landscape has been forming and the tables have gradually been turned. New York is now the world's number one visual arts metropolis, boasting some magnificent museums, an ever-increasing number of innovative artists and an eager, appreciative public.

The foundations were laid by the railroad kings and steel barons, as they brought back paintings and sculptures from the old world to form the basis of vast collections in the new. The Metropolitan Museum of Art benefitted from the country's insatiable desire for new cultural riches, as did the Museum of

Watching the world go by on the steps of the Metropolitan Museum of Art

Modern Art later on, to which most of the art brought back was donated. It was then just a case of sifting out the real treasures from the piles of accumulated artefacts.

And the spirit of patronage lives on. No other place in the world can boast so many wealthy collectors, and the sums they bid at such prestigious auction houses as Sotheby's and Christie's continue to escalate to staggering new heights.

Many reputable galleries are established in the city, offering contemporary artists a platform for their work. You can find out which exhibitions are all the rage and those worth a visit by looking in the newspapers. Reviews are printed in the *New York Times* on Fridays and Sundays, and in the weekly *New York Magazine, Time Out* and the *New Yorker*.

For a small fee, most museums can provide you with a personal stereo with a taped commentary that will guide you expertly around an exhibition. There is no fixed admission fee in many of the museums, but visitors are expected to pay a voluntary contribution. The

MARCO POLO SELECTION: MUSEUMS

1 American Museum of Natural History
Dinosaurs (page 34)

2 Cooper-Hewitt Museum
Design (page 35)

3 Guggenheim Museum
Art collections in Frank Lloyd Wright's building (page 36)

4 Metropolitan Museum
The Temple of Dendur, Louis C. Tiffany's windows and the Sculpture Garden (page 37)

5 Museum of Modern Art
Astounding collection of modern masterpieces (page 38)

6 National Museum of the American Indian
America's first inhabitants are honoured here (page 39)

7 Whitney Museum
Georgia O'Keefe, Edward Hopper collections and avantgarde (page 39)

---

suggested amount is usually displayed somewhere near the entrance. Remember that most of the museums in New York are closed on Mondays.

American Craft Museum (105/F4)

The museum's permanent collection and its frequent temporary exhibitions are all devoted to traditional American arts and crafts. It's worth coming here just to admire the exhibition space: a three-storey atrium, with a suspended white wooden staircase. *Tues, Wed, Fri-Sun 10.00-18.00, Thurs 10.00-20.00; admission: $5; 40 West 53rd Street, between 5th and 6th Avenue; Tel: 956-3535; Subway: 47th-50th Street, B, D, F, Q*

American Museum of the Moving Image (O)

This institution for film enthusiasts has two cinemas which screen highly selective retrospectives. The building was opened in 1920 by Paramount Pictures as its studios for the last silent movies and first talkies and wel-

comed such stars as the Marx Brothers and Rudolph Valentino. The Museum's basic collection holds about 60,000 objects, including costumes, scenery, posters and magazines. *Tues-Fri 12.00-17.00, Sat/Sun 11.00-18.00; admission: $8; 3601 35th Avenue, between 36th Street and 37th Street, Queens; Tel: 784-0077; Subway: Steinway Street, R (only on weekdays)*

American Museum of Natural History (101/E6)

★ This museum west of Central Park has an incredible 36 million artefacts, including a 27m (90 ft) blue whale skeleton, the largest sapphire in the world (563 carats), the biggest meteorites and the most extensive collection of dinosaur skeletons (on the fourth floor, which has just been completely renovated). The third floor exhibits small scenes from the everyday life of North American Indians, re-created down to the last detail. The newly-built *Hall of*

34

Biodiversity is dedicated to the evolution of various organisms, and *Habitats of the World* presents nine ecosystems. The exhibits on the lower two floors are based on the themes of nature, physics and ethnic cultures and there are four gift shops selling a wide variety of original souvenirs (Indian jewellery, dinosaur T-shirts and flying dragons). 'Naturemax', the IMAX cinema with the largest screen in New York, and the 'Hayden Planetarium', where a three-dimensional laser show is put on, are closed until the year 2000.
Sun-Thurs 10.00-17.45, Fri/Sat 10.00-20.45; admission free Fri and Sat after 20.00; Central Park West/ 79th Street; Tel: 769-5100; Subway: 81st Street, B, C

The Museum of Natural History

Brooklyn Museum (O)

An excellent reason for taking a trip out to Brooklyn is to visit the Brooklyn Museum and the neighbouring Brooklyn Botanic Garden. The turn-of-the-century building that houses the museum was designed by New York architects McKim, Mead & White and, with over two mil-

lion objects, has the seventh largest art collection in America. As it is bursting at the seams, there are plans afoot for an extension. If you visit the museum, the Egyptian collection (third floor) and the pre-Columbian collection (first floor) are a must. In the Period Rooms (fourth floor), over 20 sitting rooms and dining rooms from New England houses between 1675 and 1830 have been re-created. The American collection (fifth floor) provides a broad view of American art. An amazing 58 sculptures by Rodin are displayed in the Iris and Gerald Cantor Gallery, and a collection of architectural ornamentation taken from New York buildings demolished this century has been laid out in the Sculpture Garden at the back of the museum. *Daily (except Mon and Tues) 10.00-17.00; 200 Eastern Parkway, Brooklyn; Tel: 638-5000; Subway: Eastern Parkway, 2, 3*

Cooper-Hewitt Museum (102/A4)

★ This 64-room townhouse was built in 1901 and was formerly home to the industrialist Andrew Carnegie. Luckily it has not succumbed to the fate of being turned into an apartment complex. It houses an excellent collection of textiles, furniture, glass, ceramics and metal ornaments and is New York's specialist museum of design and decorative art. The exquisitely decorated Tiffany-Baldachin above the entrance made of copper and bronze gives you a foretaste of some of the most beautiful artefacts you'll ever see. The temporary exhibitions are all devoted to the world of design. *Tues 10.00-21.00, Wed-Sat 10.00-17.00, Sun 12.00-17.00;*

2 East 91st Street; Tel: 860-6868; Subway: 86th Street, 4, 5, 6

Frick Collection (106/A2)

The Beaux-Arts mansion of the industrialist Henry Clay Frick houses a small collection, providing an informative glimpse into the world of rich American art collectors: paintings by Rembrandt, Holbein, Vermeer, Fragonard and Renoir and furniture from the period of Louis XV and Louis XVI are but a few of the items on view. The Frick is also worth a visit for the building itself. It was converted into a museum in 1935 and the stunning gardens complete with fountains, ionic columns and stone benches provide a haven in the midst of Manhattan's traffic turmoil. Temporary exhibitions are held here on a regular basis. *Tues-Sat 10.00-18.00, Sun 13.00-18.00; admission: $5; 1 East 70th Street/5th Avenue; Tel: 288-0700; Subway: 68th Street, 6*

Guggenheim Museum (102/A5)

★ The unconventional building designed by the great American architect Frank Lloyd Wright, described by critics as a 'concrete saucer', is one of the city's most famous structures. Temporary exhibitions of contemporary art are set up along the 364 m (1200 ft) spiral ramp that winds its way up from street level to the fourth floor. Some of the museum's permanent collections include works by artists such as Mondrian, Braque, Modigliani, Kandinsky, Malevich and Klee. Or you may feast your eyes on the exceptional Thannhauser collection, consisting of, among others, Van Gogh's *Mountains of Saint Rémy*,

Cézanne's mystifying *Man with Crossed Arms* and Camille Pissarro's 1867 landscape entitled *The Hermitage at Pontoise*. In the summer of 1992, the long awaited extension, custom built for the collection of copper magnate Solomon Guggenheim, was completed (mainly paintings by Van Gogh, Monet, Degas and Pablo Picasso). Nice café and shop selling art books. *Sun-Wed 10.00-18.00, Fri/Sat 10.00-20.00; admission: $10; 1071 5th Avenue/88th to 89th Street; Tel: 423-3500; Subway: 86th Street, 4, 5, 6*

The Guggenheim Museum SoHo (114/B1) holds temporary exhibitions of works by young artists. Good gift shop. *Sun, Wed-Fri 11.00-18.00, Sat 11.00-20.00; admission: $8; 575 Broadway/Prince Street; Subway: Prince Street, R*

International Center of Photography (102/A4)

This comparatively young art form is carefully nurtured here with exhibitions by reputed photographers and up-and-coming talents. It has a bookshop with a wide selection of postcards and books on photography. *Tues 11.00-20.00, Wed-Sun 11.00-18.00; admission: $4; 1130 5th Avenue/ 94th Street; Tel: 860-1777; Subway: 96th Street, 6*

Intrepid Sea-Air-Space Museum (104/C5)

On deck of this aircraft carrier which was brought into action in World War II and in the Vietnam Wars, you can take a look at combat aircrafts. You can also see a submarine and exhibitions on aircraft design. *In summer: Mon-Fri 10.00-17.00, Sat / Sun 10.00-18.00; in winter: Wed-Sun 10.00-17.00; admission: $10; Pier 86,*

12th Avenue at 46th Street; Tel. 245-0072; Subway: 50th Street, A, C

Isamu Noguchi
Garden Museum (107/E1)

The old studio of sculptor Isamu Noguchi – a former light factory in Queens – has been converted into 12 exhibition rooms and gardens arranged in order of subject, providing an overview of the artist's impressive work.

April to Oct, Wed-Fri Sat/Sun 10.00-17.00; admission $4; 32-37 Vernon Boulevard, Long Island City, Queens; Tel: 204-7088; bus (only Sat and Sun) from Asia Society, 725 Park Avenue/70th Street, every hour between 11.30 and 15.30; $5

Jacques Marchais
Center of Tibetan Art (O)

This mountain temple replica stands in the middle of terraced gardens with a lush lotus pool, which afford a wonderful view over New York Bay. A collection of artefacts related to Buddhism, including an altar with prayer wheels, is housed within.

From April to November: Wed-Sun 13.00-17.00; admission: $3; 338 Lighthouse Avenue, Richmondtown, Staten Island; Tel: 987-3500; Bus No. 74 from Staten Island Ferry Terminal, get off at Lighthouse Avenue

Metropolitan
Museum of Art (102/A5–6)

★ The imposing grey sandstone façade of this museum, built in 1870, was designed by Richard Morris Hunt in 1902. ☀ A constant throng mills about the huge flight of steps that lead up to the entrance. A great place to sit down, relax and watch the comings and goings. There's not a lot left to see of the original building.

New York's most famous museum is expanding from all four corners: extensions are being built into the surrounding Central Park. At present, only a quarter of the collection's 3.2 million artefacts can be displayed in the 40 acres of exhibiting space. Regular temporary exhibitions featuring the life's work of artists or work representing whole periods restrict the available space yet further. You'll need about two two-hour trips to visit the permanent exhibition. On your first visit, you should take in the Egyptian wing (ground floor to the right) with the Temple of Dendur which was rescued from submersion during the construction of the Aswan High dam, and completely reconstructed. This should be followed by a visit to the American Wing around Engelhard Court with its windows, lamps and silver from Louis Comfort Tiffany's estate, and the 20 period rooms each representing a different era (including one designed by Frank Lloyd Wright, to demonstrate to his clients how best to design a room in line with his architectural style). Your second visit should include the collection of primitive art in the Michael C. Rockefeller Wing and the display of modern American art in the ↯ Sculpture Garden on the roof. The roof garden, open from April to October, is worth a detour both for its modern sculptures and for the view over Central Park and the midtown Manhattan skyline. The museum also boasts Greek and Roman art, 13th-century European paintings, Eastern and Islamic art, musical instruments, arms and armour, drawings, prints and photographs, as well as a section devoted entirely to costume which comprises 40,000 items of clothing spanning five centuries, from all five continents. The museum shops on the ground floor offer a varied selection of gifts and souvenirs, including art books. The restaurant in the Great Hall serves a wide range of refreshments, from iced tea and sandwiches to a three-course meal. After 5 pm on Fridays and Saturdays, you can have drinks on the balcony accompanied by chamber music.

Tues-Thurs and Sun 9.30-17.15, Fri/Sat 9.30-20.45; admission: $8; 5th Avenue and 82nd Street; Tel: 535-7710; Subway: 86th Street, 4, 5, 6

Museum of American Folk Art (105/E2)

A wonderful collection of folk art and handicrafts. Exhibits include saddlecloths that once belonged to Indian chiefs, quilts, intricate patchwork covers, decoys, old wooden horses and much more. The museum's present location is temporary as it's to be relocated in 1999 to the original building at 49 West 53rd Street.

Tues-Sun 11.30-19.30; admission $3; 2 Lincoln Square, between Columbus Avenue and 65th Street; Tel: 595-9533; Subway: 66th Street, 1, 9

Museum of Modern Art (105/F4)

★ This is often described as the best museum of its kind. A two- to three-hour visit will give you a good overview of 20th-century art, with master pieces such as Claude Monet's *Waterlilies*, Picasso's *Les Demoiselles d'Avignon* and Andrew Wyeth's *Christina's World*. The building was opened in 1939 and renovated by Philip Johnson in 1964 (then also curator of the museum's design department). An extension designed by Cesar Pelli was added in 1984. The overall effect creates an impression of light and space, showing the works of art to their best advantage. The museum houses a collection containing over 100,000 artefacts, including 3500 paintings and sculptures, 2200 design objects, 40,000 prints, 20,000 drawings, 20,000 photographs and 9000 cinema films. The inner courtyard filled with birch trees is known as the Sculpture Garden; here you can see Picasso's *She-Goat* and Max Ernst's chess sculpture *King Playing with Queen* which he designed in 1944 while in exile in America. From this courtyard, in the midst of great works of art and gushing water fountains which almost succeed in drowning out the noise of the traffic, you can enjoy the ◁▷ panorama of surrounding skyscrapers.

All the big names are on the second floor: Monet, Mondrian, Matisse, Kandinsky, Klee, Picasso and Miró are displayed in separate rooms. Some rooms are devoted to the principal movements: Cubism, Expressionism, Futurism, Post-Impressionism, Constructivism and Surrealism, and there's a separate department for photography. The third floor covers contemporary painting and sculpture, Abstract Expressionism and prewar American art, and it is also where Wyeth's *Christina's World* hangs. Finally, on the fourth floor, you'll come to the museum's famous architectural and design collection which

includes a helicopter suspended from the ceiling and a 1946 Cisitalia. The temporary exhibitions, usually held on the ground floor, are critically acclaimed worldwide and should not be missed. The 'Sette Motta' restaurant and the second floor bookshop are well worth a visit.
Sat-Tue, Thurs 10.30-18.00, Fri 10.30-18.30; admission: $9.50 (Fri after 17.30 free); 11 West 53rd Street, between 5th and 6th Avenue; Tel: 708-9400; Subway: 47th-50th Street, B, D, F, Q

Museum of Television and Radio (105/F4)

Unusual retrospectives are screened in the in-house cinema. Extracts from over 20,000 television programmes kept in the museum's archives can be viewed on small screens.
Tues-Su 12.00-18.00, Thurs 12.00-20.00; admission: $6; 25 West 52nd Street, between 5th and 6th Avenue; Tel: 621-6600; Subway: 47th-50th Street, B, D, F, Q

National Museum of the American Indian (114/B6)

★ A selection of the three million native American objects collected by New York banker George Gustav Heye – carpets, baskets, pottery and photos – are displayed on two floors of the former U.S. Custom House at the southern tip of Manhattan. Temporary exhibitions, which are regularly shown, also provide budding native American artists with a platform for their work. *Fri-Wed 10.00-17.00, Thurs 10.00-20.00; One Bowling Green (bordering Battery Park); Tel: 668-6624; Subway: South Ferry, 1, 9*

New Museum of Contemporary Art (114/B1)

Only the very latest avant-garde talent is displayed here, and no more than two artists exhibit their work at any one time. The museum is well worth a visit and is also an excellent stop-off point when touring the SoHo galleries.
Wed-Fri, Sun 12.00-18.00, Sat 12.00-20.00; admission: $4; 583 Broadway, between Houston and Prince Street; Tel: 219-1222; Subway: Prince Street, R

Whitney Museum of American Art (106/A1)

★ Minimalist grey granite blocks, designed in the 1960s by the Bauhaus-influenced architect and designer Marcel Breuer. An extension is planned, but the design is the subject of hot dispute among enthusiasts of the museum. Two hours should be ample time to look around the Whitney, which devotes its four floors to 20th-century American art. The collection includes paintings by, among others, Edward Hopper, Georgia O'Keeffe and Jasper Johns, but unfortunately it is not always possible to view them. Every two years in May, the 'Whitney Biennial of American Art' – a highly informative overview of the latest developments in contemporary art – is held here. There's a gift shop on the ground floor that stocks art books and exhibition catalogues from all over America. Cafeteria in the basement.
Wed, Fri-Sun 11.00-18.00, Thurs 13.00-20.00; admission: $8; 945 Madison Avenue/75th Street; Tel: 570-3676; Subway: 77th Street, 6

Cosmopolitan cuisine

Italian, Japanese, Creole, French, 'nouvelle American'…
eat your way around the world!

Life in New York is lived in the fast lane. Everyone is in a hurry and those who live and work here seem to find little time for relaxing during their busy working week. Lunch hours are frequently skipped and often consist of a quick sandwich eaten on the hop. In the evenings, if you don't eat out, dinner is frequently a pre-prepared frozen meal cooked in the microwave. That isn't to say that New Yorkers don't have their own culinary culture and a taste for more refined cuisine. The city is overflowing with good restaurants. There are plenty of opportunities to indulge the appetite with classic exotic food and wine in French or Italian style, but it can be very expensive and there are lots of other exciting, and less costly, alternatives. If you too are pressed for time during your busy touring schedule, there is no shortage of fast-food joints, Chinese restaurants or pizzerias where you can grab a quick snack or take-away. Alternatively you

can go to a coffee shop or diner. Coffee shops (not to be confused with the new espresso bars that are cropping up everywhere in response to the demand for good, strong coffee) are typically American. They serve food with 'bottomless' filter coffee: you can have as many refills as you like for the price of one cup. If you look hard enough, you can still find coffee shops offering a full breakfast, including eggs, for under $5. Lunches and dinners are served all day long in most coffee shops and diners, many of which are open 24 hours a day.

The word 'restaurant' is applied liberally in America, and is even used to refer to snack bars and food stands. 'Proper' restaurants have a *maître d'* who greets customers and allocates tables – you very rarely choose your own.

The tip should be more than just an appreciative gesture as it is part of the waiting staff's wages. On top of the 8.25% local sales tax you should add at least 15% to the menu prices. When paying in cash, just put the money on the table as you leave. If you pay by credit card, remember to enter

Chinatown – for delicious food at a cheap price

the discretionary service charge in the designated section on the slip, or someone may well do it for you!

The range of restaurants in New York is vast and covers all four corners of the globe: Thai, Chinese, Vietnamese, Japanese (sushi has been fashionable food for some years), Mexican and Indian are all well represented. Caribbean, Creole and Malay cuisines are also worth sampling.

New Yorkers don't just go out to eat; they go out to spy. One sees the newest fashion trends at the next table, and gets an earful of the latest gossip (entirely accidentally, of course).

Tourists, on the other hand, are to be lured by entertainment. For instance, horrors for teenagers young and old are served up at the *Jekyll & Hyde Club (1409 6th Avenue/57th Street; Tel: 541-9505)*. Sixties music is on the menu at

the *Motown Café (104 West 57th Street/6th Avenue; Tel: 581-8030)*. And a biker wind blows in the *Harley Davidson Café (1370 6th Avenue; Tel: 245-6000)*.

Micro breweries are a new trend, featuring various kinds of beer that are brewed in-house. The atmosphere is comfortable, and the food is simple, good and usually cheap. There are pubs such as *Heartland Brewery (5 Union Square West/17th Street; Tel: 645-3400)* as well as giants like *Hansen's Times SquareBrewery (160 West 42nd Street/Broadway; Tel: 398-1234)*.

The *Chelsea Market* is a recent addition to the local shopping scene; its 18 shops (offering everything from ice cream to sourdough bread) give a good overview of first-class New York products. One can sample as well as buy. *75 9th Avenue/15th Street; Tel: 243-6005*.

MARCO POLO SELECTION: RESTAURANTS

1 Chanterelle
Creative French cuisine in a converted downtown loft (page 44)

2 Gotham Bar & Grill
Dine in style in this former warehouse (page 47)

3 Jojo
Heavenly cuisine at down-to-earth prices (page 43)

4 Nobu
Elegant Japanese restaurant with chic clientele (page 44)

5 The Palm Court
Brunch in The Plaza hotel (page 45)

6 Remi
A first-rate Italian restaurant (page 48)

7 Republic
Asian cuisine served on large tables (page 51)

8 Sylvia's Restaurant
Breakfast in Harlem (page 51)

9 Time Café
Downtown, it's the 'in' place to be, and the pizza is excellent (page 48)

10 Vong
Thai restaurant with wonderful decor (page 45)

Here is a selection of some of the best restaurants in New York, categorized according to price.

RESTAURANTS

Category 1
Three-course meal from $50 per person.

Café des Artistes (105/E2)
French restaurant. Romantic atmosphere, murals and floral arrangements. Good cuisine near Lincoln Center. Sunday brunch.
Mon-Sat 12.00-15.00, 17.30-24.00, Sun 10.00-15.00, 17.00-23.00; 1 West 67th Street, between Central Park West and Columbus Avenue; Tel: 877-3500; Subway: 66th Street, 1, 9

Il Cantinori (110/A5)
Tuscan-style country house with such prominent guests as Richard Gere. Pasta, game, fish.
Mon-Fri 12.00-14.30, daily 18.00-23.00; 32 East 10th Street, between University Place and Broadway; Tel: 673-6044; Subway: 8th Street, N, R

Les Célébrités (105/F3)
Exotic Franco-American fare as 'Foie Gras Burger' served on a bed of apples, in luxurious and theatrical surroundings.
Tues-Thurs 18.00-22.00, Fri/Sat 17.30-22.30; 155 West 58th Street, between 6th and 7th Avenue; Tel: 484-5113; Subway: 57th Street, B, N, R, Q

Four Seasons (106/A4)
A luncheon haunt for publishing, theatre and art scene managers. Oysters, superior hamburgers.
Mon-Fri 12.00-14.00 and 17.00-22.00; Sat 17.00-23.00; 99 East 52nd Street, between Lexington and Park Avenue; Tel: 754-9494; Subway: 51st Street, 6

Hatsuhana (106/A5)
The sushi and sashimi are among the best in the city. A good value lunchtime special is available from $18.50.
Mon-Fri 11.45-14.30, Mon-Sat 17.30-21.45; 17 East 48th Street, between 5th and Madison Avenue; Tel: 355-3345; Subway: 51st Street, 6

Jojo (106/B3)
★ Chef Jean-Georges Vongerichten cooks light French cuisine with Thai accents. Good appetizers such as tuna-fish spring rolls.
Mon-Fri 12.00-14.30, Mon-Sat 18.00-23.00; 160 East 64th Street/ Lexington Avenue; Tel: 223-5656; Subway: 68th Street, 6

Kokachin (106/A4)
Chef Elka Gilmore dishes up outstanding fish, often raw. Try bar area tables for exquisite snacks.
Mon-Fri 12.00-14.00 and 17.30-22.00; 21 East 52nd Street/Madison Avenue; Tel: 355-9300; Subway: 51st Street, 6

Mark's (102/A6)
Atmosphere reminiscent of an old English club. Savour a classic (oysters, steak) or the unusual like *Vintner's Garden:* appropriate wines served with each course.
Daily 11.30-14.30 and 18.30-22.30; 25 East 77th Street, between Madison and 5th Avenue; Tel: 879-1864; Subway: 77th Street, 6

Palio (105/F4)
Refined Italian cuisine. Tip: one of the eight tables in the bar area beneath the Sandro Chia painting. Background music: classical.
Mon-Fri 12.30-14.00 and 17.30-

The Gourmet Palaces of New York

Chanterelle (114/A3)

★ Innovative cuisine in a converted loft in TriBeCa. Try the salmon ravioli on a bed of cabbage, sprinkled with caviar. Menu from $75. Reserve well in advance.
Tues-Sat 12.00-14.30 and 18.00-22.30; 2 Harrison Street/Hudson Street; Tel: 966-6960; Subway: Franklin Street, 1, 9

Le Cirque 2000 (106/A5)

Besides the goose liver ravioli and the lobster risotto, the patrons (many of whom are famous) are an attraction here. Summer garden! Dinner $90.
Daily 11.45.-14.00 and 17.45-22.30; 455 Madison Avenue/ 50th Stree; Tel: 303-7788; Subway: 51st Street, 6

Daniel (106/A1)

Upper East Side society gather here for oyster soup with caviar, followed by scallops or sea bass in a potato crust. First-rate wine list. Set menu (a selection of 8 dishes) $110.
Tues-Fri 12.00-14.15, Mon-Sat 17.45-23.30; 20 East 76th Street/Madison Avenue; Tel: 288-0033; Subway: 77th Street, 6

Fiftyseven Fiftyseven (106/A3)

Located in the Four Seasons Hotel. There's an excellent Caesar's Salad with lobster, and a 'martini card' with 12 varieties. Meals with wine start at $75. *Open daily 11.30-14.00 and 18-22.30. 57 East 57th Street/Madison Avenue; Tel: 758-5757; Subway: 59th Street, 4, 5, 6*

Jean-Georges (105/E3)

Star chef Vongerichten presents a fascinating range of offerings full of exotic taste combinations. Meals about $105. Less expensive: ordering à la carte in the garden during summer.
Daily 12.00-14.30 and 17.30-23.00; 1 Central Park West/60th Street; Tel: 299-3900; Subway: Columbus Circle, A, B, C, D, 1, 9

Lespinasse (106/A4)

Light, exotic and inspirational dishes, such as lamb cutlets in a curried carrot sauce, prepared by Gray Kunz. Excellent desserts. Set menu: $130.
Mon-Sat 12.00-14.00 and 18.00-22.00; 2 East 55th Street; Tel: 339-6719; Subway: 5th Avenue, N, R

Lutèce (106/B5)

Located in an old New York townhouse, this restaurant is the place to savour modern French cuisine as prepared by innovative chef Eberhard Müller. Set menu (consists of 6 courses) $85.
Tues-Fri 12.00-13.45, Mon-Sat 17.30-22.00; 249 East 50th Street; between 2nd and 3rd Avenue; Tel: 752-2225/26; Subway: 51st Street, 6

Nobu (114/A2)

★ High-class Japanese fare, with outstanding sashimi, sushi and zempura. If you pick Omakase, you leave the choice of dishes to Chef Nobu ($60). Reservations are made with the concierge!
Mon-Fri 11.45-14.00, daily 17.45-22.00; 105 Hudson Street/ Franklin Street; Tel: 219-0500; Subways: Franklin Street, 1, 9

23.00, Sat 17.30-23.30; 151 West 51st Street, between 6th and 7th Avenue; Tel: 245-4850; Subway: 47th-50th Street, B, D, F, Q

The Palm Court (106/A3)
★ The best brunch in town, in The Plaza hotel. Oysters, shrimps, salmon, roast beef and more.
($44.75, Sun 10.00-14.30) daily 07.00-24.00; 768 5th Avenue; Tel: 546-5350; Subway: 5th Avenue, N, R

Patria (110/A3)
Latino cuisine, including a tunafish steak speared on a piece of sugar cane; lively ambience.
Mon-Fri 12.00-15.00, daily 17.30-23.00; 250 Park Avenue South/20th Street; Tel: 777-6211; Subway: 23rd Street, 6

The Rainbow Room (105/F5)
◀▶ Plush restaurant on the 65th floor of the GE Building in Rockefeller Center with splendid view over the city. Recommended: an appetizer with your drink at the bar *(the Rainbow Promenade).*
Tues-Sat 17.30-24.00; 30 Rockefeller Plaza, between 49th and 50th Street; Tel: 632-5100; Subway: 47th-50th Street, B, D, F, Q

The River Café (115/E4)
Restaurant on a barge moored under the Brooklyn Bridge. Great view of Manhattan's skyline. In summer, sip your drinks on the terrace. Creative American cuisine. Recommendation: Saturday and Sunday brunch *(12.00 to 14.30).*
Mon-Fri 12.00-14.30 and 18.00-23.00, Sun 18.30-22.30; One Water Street/Old Fulton Street, Brooklyn; Tel: 522-5200; Subway: Clark Street, 2, 3

Verbena (110/B4)
Located in the romantic Irving Place Inn. Very fresh ingredients. Inner courtyard open in summer.
Tues-Fri, Sun 12.00-14.30, daily 17.30-22.00; 54 Irving Place/17th Street; Tel: 260-5454; Subway: Union Square, L, N, R, 4, 5, 6

Vong (106/B4)
★ Thai cuisine in sumptuous red and gold decor that would do any stage set credit. Chef's specialities include lobster with Thai herbs.
Mon-Fri 12.00-14.30, Mon-Sat 18.00-23.00, Sun 17.30-22.00; 200 East 54th Street/3rd Avenue; Tel: 486-9592; Subway: 51st Street, 6

Category 2
Three-course meal between $25 and $50 per person.

Aquagrill (114/A1)
First-class fish restaurant with a good oyster bar. In SoHo.
Tues-Fri 12.00-15.00, Tues-Thurs, Sun 18.00-22.45; 210 Spring Street/Avenue of the Americas; Tel: 274-0505; Subway; Spring Street, C, E

Arqua (114/B2)
Elegant loft in TriBeCa serving Venetian specialities.
Mon-Fri 12.00-15.00, Mon-Sat 17.30-22.00; 281 Church Street/White Street; Tel: 334-1888; Subway: Canal Street, 1, 9

Benny Benson (105/F4)
Good steakhouse with gigantic portions. Only if you're very hungry or plan to share.
Mon-Fri 12.00-23.00, Sat/Sun 17.00-24.00; 123 West 52nd Street, between 6th and 7th Avenue; Tel: 581-8888; Subway: 47th-50th Street, B, D, F, Q

Bryant Park Grill **(105/F6)**
This restaurant behind the Public Library is a popular meeting place for models and fashion writers. Summer terrace. Sunday brunch.
Daily 11.30-15.30 and 17.30-23.30; 25 West 40th Street, between 5th and 6th Avenue; Tel: 840-6500; Subway: 42nd Street, B, D, F, Q

China Grill **(105/F4)**
Cal-Asian (Californian-Asian) cuisine, e.g. tuna-fish tempura or Peking-style duck pancakes.
Mon-Fri 11.45-17.00 and 17.30-23.00, Sat 17.30-24.00, Sun 18.00-22.00; 60 West 53rd Street/6th Avenue; Tel: 333-7788; Subway: 47th-50th Street, B, D, F, Q

Coffee Shop **(110/A4)**
✝ The Brazilian-inspired cuisine in this coffee shop draws a trendy downtown crowd.
Mon-Fri 06.30-05.30, Sat 08.00-05.30, Sun 08.00-02.00; 29 Union Square/16th Street; Tel: 243-7969; Subway: 14th Street/Union Square, 4, 5, 6, N, R

Le Colonial **(106/B3)**
Food and decor reminiscent of Saigon in the 1960s. Stylish bar.
Mon-Fri 12.00-14.30, daily 17.30-23.00; 149 East 57th Street, between 3rd and Lexington Avenue; Tel: 752-0808; Subway: 59th Street, 4, 5, 6, N, R

Dock's **(106/B6)**
Lively fish restaurant with 'catch of the day' dishes.
Mon-Fri 11.30-23.00, Sat 17.00-24.00, Sun 11.30-15.00 and 17.00-23.00; 633 3rd Avenue/40th Street; Tel: 986-8080; Subway: 42nd Street/Grand Central, 4, 5, 6

44 **(105/F5)**
✝ Exciting new American cuisine served in the stylish lobby of the Hotel Royalton. Brunch served on weekends.
Mon-Fri 12.00-15.00, daily 17.45-22.45, Sat/Sun brunch 11.00-15.00; 44 West 44th Street, between 5th and 6th Avenue; Tel: 944-8844; Subway: 42nd Street/Times Square, 1, 2, 3, 9, N, R

Frank's **(109/D4)**
Eccentric steak restaurant and bar, on the edge of the slaughterhouse district. Speciality: the Shell Steak ($29).
Mon-Fri 10.30-23.00, Sat 17.00-23.00; 85 10th Avenue/15th Street; Tel: 243-1349; Subway:14th Street, A, C, E

Ordering correctly

Whoever wants to order America's popular egg and meat dishes in a restaurant must know how. With eggs, Americans distinguish between scrambled, sunny side up (fried), over easy (lightly fried on both sides) or poached. You can have your steak, hamburger and tuna-fish dishes served *rare* (bloody red), *medium rare* (quickly grilled), *medium well* (half-done), and *well-done* (cooked through). As for drinks: If you want ice, order *on the rocks*. Pure is referred to as *straight up* or *neat*. A drink with ice that has been crushed and mixed in a blender is called *frozen*.

Fu's (106/B4)
One of the best Chinese restaurants in the city. Szechuan.
Daily 12.00-23.30; 972 2nd Avenue, between 51st and 52nd Street; Tel: 421-2322; Subway: 51st Street, 6

Gabriel's (105/E3)
Chic Italian restaurant near Lincoln Center.
Mon-Fri 12.00-15.00 and 17.30-23.00; 11 West 60th Street/ Broadway; Tel: 956-4600; Subway: Columbus Circle, A, C, D, 1

Gotham Bar & Grill (110/A4)
★ Loft with excellent American cuisine, exceptional service. Popular with photographers.
Mon-Fri 12.00-14.00, Sun-Thurs 17.30-22.00, Fri/Sat 17.30-23.00; 12 East 12th Street, between 5th Avenue and University Place; Tel: 620-4020; Subway: 14th Street/ Union Square, 4, 5, 6, N, R

Les Halles (110/A2)
Meat dishes, prepared in the best French tradition.
Daily 12.00-24.00; 411 Park Avenue, between 28th and 29th Street; Tel: 679-4111; Subway: 28th Street, 6

Lucky Strike (114/B2)
⚖ Loud and lively, brasserie-style place with young clientele.
Daily 12.00-04.00; 59 Grand Street, between West Broadway and Wooster Street; Tel: 941-0479; Subway: Canal Street, 1, 9

Le Madri (109/E4)
A wonderfully chic restaurant that serves delicious Tuscan food.
Daily 12.00-15.00 and 18.00-23.30; 168 West 18th Street/ 7th Avenue; Tel: 727-8022; Subway: 18th Street, 1, 9

A street café in South Street Seaport

Mesa Grill (110/A4)
Hot and imaginative; the 'in' restaurant of the Flat Iron district.
Mon-Fri 12.00-14.15, Sat/Sun 11.30-15.00, daily 17.30-22.30; 102 5th Avenue/15th Street; Tel: 807-7400; Subway: 14th Street/ Union Square, 4, 5, 6, L, N, R

Odeon (114/B3)
⚖ Upmarket bistro with *art deco* design. A nocturnals' favourite.
Daily 12.00-02.00, Sun brunch 11.30-16.00; 145 West Broadway/ Thomas Street; Tel: 233-0507; Subway: Chambers Street, 1, 2, 3, 9, A, C

Osteria del Circo (105/F4)
Venetian cuisine under a circus dome design. Lively bar near the Theater District.
Daily 11.30-15.00 and 17.30-23.00; 120 West 55th Street/Avenue of the Americas; Tel: 265-3636; Subway: 57th Street, N, R

Oyster Bar (106/A6)
In Grand Central Station. Feast on a dozen different types of oyster, pan roast, lobster soup and fresh fish.
Mon-Fri 11.30-21.30; Grand Central Station, Lower Level, between Vanderbilt and Lexington Avenue;

Tel: 490-6650; Subway: Grand Central, 4, 5, 6, 7

Peter Luger (O)
Steakhouse with lots of charm, and large portions too.
Mon-Thurs 11.45-21.45, Fri/Sat until 23.00, Sun 13.00-21.45; 178 Broadway, between Driggs and Bedford Street, Brooklyn; Tel: 387-7400; Subway: Marcy Avenue, J

Raoul (114/A1)
SoHo bistro frequented by arty types; loud and smoky.
Sun-Thurs 18.00-24.00, Fri/Sat until 02.00; 180 Prince Street, between Sullivan and Thompson Street; Tel: 966-3518; Subway: Spring Street, C, E

Remi (105/F4)
★ Smart, unusually designed Italian restaurant; in the courtyard opposite there's a stand called 'Remi to go'.
Mon-Fri 12.00-14.30, daily 17.30-23.30; 145 West 53rd Street, between 6th and 7th Avenue; Tel: 581-4242; Subway: 50th Street, 1, 9

The Sea Grill (105/F5)
✌ In winter, look out onto the ice-skaters in Rockefeller Cente; in summer, onto bustling café tables. Good fish dishes.
Mon-Fri 12.00-15.00, Mon-Sat 17.00-22.00; 19 West 49th Street, between 5th and 6th Avenue; Tel: 332-7610; Subway: 47th-50th Streets, B, D, F, Q

Tavern on the Green (105/E2)
✌ Under open skies in Central Park. Ideal for a drink or a meal.
Mon-Fri 11.30-15.30 and 17.00-23.00, Sat/Sun 10.00-15.30, Sat 17.00-23.30, Sun 17.00-22.30; Central Park West/67th Street; Tel: 873-3200; Subway: 72nd Street, B, C

Time Café (110/B6)
★ ☆ Loud and lively, this trendy downtown eatery serves good pizza, pasta and salmon. Good place to spot models and fashion celebrities. Performance space with live music.
Daily 12.00-24.00; 380 Lafayette Street/Great Jones Street; Tel: 533-7000; Subway: Astor Place, 6

Relax in the Central Park greenery at the Boathouse Café (near 72nd Street)

Trattoria dell'Arte (105/E4)
Visit the antipasti bar in this trattoria for a bite to eat before or after the theatre.
Daily 11.45-15.30 and 17.00-23.30, Sun brunch 11.45-15.30; 900 7th Avenue, between 56th and 57th Street; Tel: 245-9800; Subway: 57th Street, N, R

TriBeCa Grill (114/A3)
Robert De Niro's American bistro is popular with fellow celebrities.
Mon-Fri 12.00-14.30, daily 17.30-23.00; 375 Greenwich Street at the corner of Franklin Street; Tel: 941-3900; Subway: Franklin Street, 1, 9

Typhoon Brewery (106/A4)
Thai food with beer brewed on the premises.
Mon-Fri 12.00-14.30, Mon-Thurs 17.30-22.30, Fri/Sat 17.30-23.30; 22 East 54th Street/Madison Avenue; Tel: 754-9006; Subway: 51st Street, E, F

Union Square Café (110/A4)
✴ Californian bistro that attracts a hip young crowd. Good bar food.
Mon-Sat 12.00-14.30 and 18.00-23.00, Sun 18.00-23.00; 21 East 16th Street, between 5th Avenue and Union Square West; Tel: 243-4020; Subway: 14th Street/ Union Square, 4, 5, 6, N, R

Zoë (114/B1)
✴ Innovative cuisine in SoHo. Try the smoked salmon with Japanese potatoes or the lamb with gnocchi.
Daily 12.00-15.00 and 18.00-22.30, 90 Prince Street/Mercer Street; Tel: 966-6722; Subway: Prince Street, R, N

Category 3
Three-course meal under $25.

Becco (105/E5)
Good pasta supper for just $19.95 in the Theater District.
Mon-Sat 12.00-15.00 and 17.00-24.00, Sun 12.00-22.30; 355 West 46th Street/9th Avenue; Tel: 397-7597; Subway: 42nd Street, A, C, E

Benny's Burritos (109/E4)
✴ Spicy Mexican food. Good burritos (filled cornmeal pancakes).
Daily 12.00-24.00; 113 Greenwich Avenue, between 7th and 8th Avenue; Tel: 727-0584; Subway: 14th Street, A, E, 1, 2, 3, 9

Bo Ky (114/C2)
Chinese-Vietnamese restaurant with plastic decor. Good soups.
Daily 08.00-21.00; 80 Bayard Street; between Mott and Mulberry Street; Tel: 406-2292; Subway: Canal Street, 6, N, R

Caffé Lure (109/F6)
✴ Good fish dishes, Italian-style.
Sun-Thurs 18.30-22.00, Sat until 24.00, Sat/Sun 10.00-15.00; 169 Sullivan Street, between Bleecker and Houston Street; Tel: 473-2642; Subway: Houston Street, 1

Carnegie Deli (105/E4)
Towering sandwiches, soups and cheesecake.
Daily 06.30-04.00; 854 7th Avenue/55th Street; Tel: 757-2245; Subway: 7th Avenue, B, D, E

Cent' Anni (109/F6)
Florentine cuisine in Greenwich Village.
Mon-Fri 12.00-15.00, daily 17.30-23.00; 50 Carmine Street, between Bleecker and Bedford Street;

Tel: 989-9494; Subway: West 4th Street, A, B, C, D, E, F, Q

Dallas BBQ (105/E1)
Barbecued spare ribs, burgers and chillies. For big appetites.
Daily 12.00-24.00; 27 West 72nd Street, between Central Park West and Columbus Avenue; Tel: 873-2004; Subway: 72nd Street, B, C

El Rio Grande (110/B1)
A restaurant divided into two: one side is Texan food (barbecued); the other, Mexican (tacos).
Daily 12.00-24.00; 160 East 38th Street, between Lexington and 3rd Avenue; Tel: 867-0922; Subway: Grand Central, 4, 5, 6, 7

Empire Diner (109/D3)
Streamlined formica and chrome design from the 1950s – a great rock-'n'-roll retro snack bar.
Open 24 hours a day; 210 10th Avenue/22nd Street; Tel: 243-2736; Subway: 23rd Street, C, E

Flamingo East (110/B4)
♣ Good bistro in garish surroundings. The fish is recommendable.
Daily 18.00-00.30; 219 2nd Avenue, between 13th and 14th Street; Tel: 533-2860; Subway: 14th Street/Union Square, 4, 5, 6, L, N, R

Florent (109/E4)
This 1940s diner has been transformed into a French bistro. Popular with rock-'n'-roll stars, models and artists.
Open 24 hours a day; 69 Gansevoort Street, between Washington and Greenwich Street; Tel: 989-5779; Subway: 14th Street, A, C, E

Ghandi (110/B-C5)
One of the best among many good Indian locales in the area.

Daily 12.00-24.00; 345 East 6th Street; between 1st and 2nd Avenue; Tel: 614-9718; Subway: Astor Place, 6

HSF (114/C2)
Chinese appetizers *(Dim Sum)* selected from the serving trolley.
Daily 07.30-02.00, dinner from 17.00; 46 Bowery/Canal Street; Tel: 374-1319; Subway: Grand Street, B, D, Q

Jean-Claude (114/B1)
♣ French restaurant with exquisite dishes. No credit cards.
Daily 18.30-23.00; 137 Sullivan Street, between Prince and Houston Street; Tel: 475-9232; Subway: Spring Street, 6

Jerry's (114/B1)
♣ Good sandwiches and grilled food. Trendy downtown scene.
Mon-Fri 09.00-11.00, daily 11.30-16.30, Mon-Sat 18.00-23.00; 101 Prince Street, between Greene and Mercer Street; Tel: 966-9464; Subway: Prince Street, N, R

Jimmy's Neutral Corner (105/F6)
Good (tuna) steaks by a former boxing coach in the Theater District.
Mon-Fri 11.00-23.00; 125 West 43rd Street, between 6th Avenue and Broadway; Tel: 764-2366; Subway: 42nd Street, B, D, F, Q

Joe's Shanghai (114/C3)
Big tables shared with other guests are the order of the day. Chinese specialities: crabs, mussels, pork. No credit cards.
Daily 11.00-22.00; 9 Pell Street/Bowery; Tel: 233-8888; Subway Grand Street, B, D, Q

John's (105/E5)
Good pizza in a former church, right in the Theater District.

Daily 11.30-23.30; 260 West 44th Street; Tel: 391-7560; Subway: 42nd Street, 1, 2, 3, N, R

Lenge (105/D2)
Stylish Japanese restaurant with good sushi and sashimi. You can make up your own combinations.
Mon-Sat 12.00-23.45, Sun 13.00-23.00; 200 Columbus Avenue/ 69th Street; Tel: 799-9188; Subway: 72nd Street, 1, 2, 3, 9

Life Bait (110/A3)
☆ A 'cool' meeting place with Southern kitchen. Delicious sweet potato chips and spicy Cajun burgers.
Mon-Sat 11.00-24.00, Sun 17.30-23.00; 14 East 23rd Street, between Broadway and Park Avenue South; Tel: 353-2400; Subway: 23rd Street, N, R

Main Street (101/D6)
For big eaters or those who share. Traditional American fare.
Mon-Sat 17.30-23.30, Sun 17.00-22.00; 446 Columbus Avenue, between 81st and 82nd Street; Tel: 873-5025; Subway: 81st Street, B, C

Oriental Garden (114/C2)
Simple and delicious fish specialities in Chinatown.
Daily 08.00-02.00; 14 Elizabeth Street, between Canal and Bayard Street; Tel: 619-0085; Subway: Canal Street, 6, N, R

Republic (110/A4)
Delicious Vietnamese cuisine. One shares large tables.
Sun-Wed 12.00-23.00, Thurs-Sat 12.00-24.00; 37 Union Square West/17th Street; Tel: 627-7172; Subway: Union Square, L, N, R, 4, 6

Roettele A.G. (110/C5)
In East Village: Sauerbraten (braised beef) with spätzle and raclette. Garden open in summer.
Mon-Sat 12.00-15.00 and 17.30-23.00; 126 East 7th Street, between 1st Avenue and Avenue A; Tel: 674-4140; Subway: Astor Place ,6

Russ and Daughter (110/C6)
The smoked salmon and buttered bagels are a must.
Mon-Sat 09.00-18.00, Sun 08.00-18.00; 179 East Houston Street/ Orchard Street; Tel: 475-4880; Subway: 2nd Avenue, F

Stage Deli (105/E4)
Enormous sandwiches named after politicians and celebrities.
Daily 06.00-01.30; 834 7th Avenue, between 53rd and 54th Street; Tel: 245-7850; Subway: 49th Street, N, R

Sylvia's Restaurant (O)
★ Southern cuisine in Harlem. New York breakfast haunt.
Mon-Sat 07.30-22.30, Sun 12.30-19.00; 328 Lenox Avenue, between 126th and 127th Street; Tel: 996-0660; Subway: 125th Street, 2, 3

Television City (105/F5)
Between burgers, you can test your talent on the silver screen.
Daily 06.30-24.00; 1250 6th Avenue/50th Street; Tel: 333-3388; Subway: 47-50th Street, B,D,F

Virgil's (105/F5)
Barbecued food roadhouse-style. Near Broadway.
Mon 11.30-23.00, Tues-Sat 11.30-24.00, Sun till 22.00; 152 West 44th Street,between 6th Avenue and Broadway; Tel: 921-9494; Subway: 42nd Street, B, D, E, Q

A shopper's paradise

You can find anything and everything in New York — if you know where to look

If you are flying to New York, leave some space in your luggage. When it's time to pack your bags for your journey home, you'll be glad of the extra room in which to squeeze all those things you couldn't resist buying. New York is full of tempting shops and you can pick up some great bargains. Tough competition has pushed prices down, so, provided the exchange rate is favourable, you can actually save money on a variety of things such as brandname jeans, laptop computers, fax machines, cameras and personal stereos. It's also worth browsing among books and CDs which are often cheaper, and there is an enormous choice of new publications and rare books.

If you have enough time and money on your hands, a trip to New York just to go shopping is well worth it. Even if you're not inclined to go on a spending spree, window shopping at some of the legendary New York stores can be just as much fun: revel in the sheer opulence of Tiffany's, the finery of Bergdorf Goodman and the megastores of such firms as Nike, Coca-Cola and Disney. Take a walk down Madison Avenue lined with top French, Italian and German designer boutiques. The East Village has achieved its own lively flair with many clothing shops for young people.

Street traders offer a large choice of books, jewellery, clothing and fashion accessories etc., while the city's picturesque flea markets are a further source of sought-after second-hand goods.

If you want to shop for everything under one roof, then take your pick of the huge department stores, all in fierce competition with one another for your custom. Bloomingdale's used to be the undisputed temple of fashion in the 1970s and 1980s, but is now fighting Macy's for pole position. The *Sales and Bargains* page in the *New York Magazine* gives good tips about special sales.

Many shops open on Sundays and don't close until 9pm on certain days of the week. Re-

Macy's on Broadway: the world's largest and most famous store

member the prices indicated don't usually include tax. Apart from food, newspapers and books, all goods are subject to an additional 8.25% local sales tax.

ANTIQUES & OLD FURNITURE

Depression Modern   (114/B1)
Reasonably priced American *art deco*.
150 Sullivan Street/West Houston Street; Subway: Spring Street, E

Lost City Arts   (114/B1)
Architectural gallery selling fittings from old NY buildings.
275 Lafayette Street, between Houston and Prince Street; Subway: Bleecker Street, 6

Manhattan Arts & Antiques Center   (106/B4)
More than 100 traders spread across three storeys.
1050 2nd Avenue, between 55th and 56th Street; Subway: 51st Street, 6

ART GALLERIES

Opening hours: 10.00-18.00. Most are closed on Mondays.

Mary Boone   (106/A4)
Helped Julian Schnabel, David Salle, Eric Fischl and others to international recognition.
745 5th Avenue/57th Street; Subway: 59th Street, 4, 5, 6, or 5th Avenue, N, R

Leo Castelli   (114/B1)
Represents the best contemporary American artists: Robert Rauschenberg, Jasper Johns, Roy Lichtenstein and Frank Stella.
420 West Broadway, between Prince & Spring Street; Subway: Prince Street, R

Paula Cooper   (109/D3)
Installations, sculptures, for example, by Jennifer Bartlett.
534 West 21st Street/10th Avenue; Subway: 23rd Street, C, E

Jay Gorney   (114/B1)
Large-scale, controversial works.
100 Greene Street, between Prince and Spring Street; Subway: Prince Street, R

Robert Miller   (106/A3)
An influential gallery, including pictures by sculptor Louise Bourgeois.
41 East 57th Street/Madison Avenue; Subway: 5th Avenue, R,N

Pace/MacGill   (106/A4)
Prestigious exhibitions of 20th-century photographic art.
32 East 57th Street, between Madison and Park Avenue; Subway: 5th Avenue, N, R

Tony Shafrazi   (114/B1)
Helped to bring graffiti artists, including Keith Haring, to fame.
119 Wooster Street, between Prince and Spring Street; Subway: Prince Street, R, or Spring Street, C, E

Holly Solomon   (114/B1)
Brightly coloured, sensational art, for example, by Nam June Paik.
172 Mercer Street/Houston Street; Subway: Prince Street, R and Bleecker Street, 6

Sonnabend   (114/B1)
Ileana Sonnabend, the former wife of Leo Castelli and 'mother' of the New York art scene, exhibits, for example works by Robert Rauschenberg.
420 West Broadway, between Prince and Spring Street; Subway: Prince Street, R, or Spring Street, C, E

MARCO POLO SELECTION: SHOPPING

1 Barney's New York
Trendy department store and
meeting place (page 56)

2 Boregaard
Designer jewellery on Madison Avenue (page 58)

3 Dean & DeLuca
Downtown delicatessen
(page 58)

4 Henri Bendel
Fashion and accessories of
the finest quality (page 57)

5 MOMA Design Store
Modern art and eye-catching
designer goods for the home
(page 58)

6 Rizzoli
Books in elegant and prestigious surroundings (page 55)

7 Takashimaya
Small department store
with classy presents and
loads of stimulating stuff
(page 57)

8 Virgin Megastore
New York's largest selection
of music (page 59)

9 Warner Bros. Studio Store
Bugs Bunny & Co. (page 58)

10 William Sonoma
A great store for the
keen cook (page 58)

BOOKS

Argosy Book Store (106/B3)
Antique books, old maps and
valuable engravings.
*116 East 59th Street, between Park and
Lexington Avenue; Subway: Lexington Avenue/59th Street, 4, 5, 6, N, R*

Barnes & Noble
♟ 15 stores for book-lovers. Computers on shop floor to check
whether a book is in stock or in
print. Seating areas for browsing.
Cafés are popular among singles.
Good value items in the *bargain
section*. International periodicals.
*675 6th Avenue, between 21st and
22nd Street; Subway: 23rd Street, 1, 9.
(109/F3); 1972 Broadway/66th Street;
Subway: 66th Street, 1, 9 (105/D2)*

Rizzoli (105/F4)
★ Browse literary works and coffee-table books to the strains of
classical music. An atmospheric,
mahogany-panelled bookshop.
*31 West 57th Street, between 5th
and 6th Avenue; Subway: 57th
Street, N, R*

CHILDREN

F.A.O. Schwarz (106/A3)
Largest selection of toys and
games in New York.
767 5th Avenue/58th Street; Subway: 5th Avenue, N, R

Hammacher Schlemmer (106/B3)
Luxury electric and electronic
goods and gadgets.
*147 East 57th Street, between Lexington and 3rd Avenue; Subway: 59th
Street, 4, 5, 6*

The Sharper Image
Unusual techno-toys and gadgets,
from golf computers to electronic
bread-slicers. Two branches.
*Pier 17, South Street Seaport; Subway:
Fulton Street, 2, 3, 4, 5 (114/B4); 4 West
57th Street, between 5th and 6th Avenue; Subway: 57th Street, B, Q (105/F4)*

CLOTHING & ACCESSORIES

Billy Martin's (106/A2)
Silver buckles, boots and stetsons for the urban cowboy.
810 Madison Avenue/68th Street; Subway: 68th Street, 6

Brooks Brothers (106/A5)
Traditional men's clothing. Shirts made from the company's own cotton fabric.
346 Madison Avenue/44th Street; Subway: Grand Central, 4, 5, 6, 7

Eddie Bauer (106/A3)
Outdoor clothes at good prices (sales!). Several locations, including: *600 Madison Avenue/58th Street; Subway: 59th Street, 4, 6*

Niketown USA (106/A4)
Nike's famous and prestigious retail outlet.
6 East 57th Street/5th Avenue; Subway: 57th Street, B, Q, N, R

Patricia Field (110/A5)
Chic downtown style for women who like to party.
10 East 8th Street/5th Avenue; Subway: 8th Street, R

Ralph Lauren (106/A1)
Classic American styles with a touch of the country.
867 Madison Avenue/72nd Street; Subway: 68th Street, 6

Reminiscence (110/A4)
New clothes made from vintage materials.
74 5th Avenue/13th Street; Subway: 14th Street, F

Screaming Mimi's (110/B6)
Second-hand gear.
382 Lafayette Street/East 4th Street; Subway: Astor Place, 6

Timberland (106/A3)
Complete outdoor collection and waterproof shoes.
709 Madison Avenue/63rd Street; Subway: 59th Street, 4, 5, 6

COSMETICS & HAIR

Frédéric Fekkai (106/A3)
Star hairstylist with famous clients. A haircut costs between $150-300!
15 West 57th Street between 5th and Madison Avenue; Tel: 753-9500; Subway: 5th Avenue, E, F

Kiehl's Pharmacy (110/B4)
Beautiful old-fashioned pharmacy with good selection of own-brand cosmetics.
109 3rd Avenue, between 13th and 14th Street; Subway: 14th Street/ Union Square, 4, 5, 6, L, N, R

Louis Licari (106/A2)
Hairdresser to the stars; specializes in colour. Clients include Madonna and Robert de Niro.
797 Madison Avenue, between 67th and 68th Street; Subway: 68th Street, 6

DEPARTMENT STORES

Barney's New York (106/A3)
★ A popular and fashionable meeting place (the basement restaurant) as well as the place to buy trendy (expensive) New York outfits. Also sells jewellery, shoes, accessories and antiques.
Mon-Fri 10.00-20.00, Sat 10.00-19.00, Sun 12.00-18.00; 660 Madison Avenue/61st Street; Subway: 59th Street, 4, 5, 6

Bergdorf Goodman (106/A3)
Wander around seven storeys of top-class designer French, Italian and young American fashion. The men's store is on

the opposite side of Fifth Avenue. *Mon-Wed, Fri/Sat 10.00-18.00, Thus 10.00-20.00; 754 5th Avenue, between 57th and 58th Streets; Subway: 5th Avenue, N, R*

Bloomingdale's (106/B3)
No longer the leading fashion house, but still merits a visit. *Mon-Fri 10.00-20.30, Sat 10.00-19.00, Sun 11.00-19.00; 1000 3rd Avenue, between 59th and 60th Street; Subway: Lexington Avenue/59th Street, 4, 5, 6, N, R*

Henri Bendel (106/A4)
★ Small, plush department store with fashion clothing and accessories sold in different boutiques within the store. *Mon-Wed, Fri/Sat 10.00-19.00, Thus 10.00-20.00, Sun 12.00-19.00; 712 5th Avenue, between 55th and 56th Street; Subway: 5th Avenue, N, R*

Macy's (109/F1)
The largest department store in the world has the largest selection of Calvin Klein jeans and offers a couple of other superlatives. Good cosmetics department. *Mon, Thurs, Fri 10.00-20.30, Tues, Wed, Sat 10.00-19.00, Sun 11.00-19.00; 151 West 34th Street/Broadway; Subway: 34th Street, B, D, F, N, Q, R*

Saks Fifth Avenue (106/A5)
High-quality American fashions. Good for men's underwear, especially boxer shorts and T-shirts. Comprehensive selection of American designers in women's department on the third floor. *Mon-Wed, Fri/Sat 10.00-18.30, Thurs 10.00-20.00, Sun 12.00-18.00; 611 5th Avenue/50th Street; Subway: 47th-50th Street, B, D, F, Q*

'Breakfast at Tiffany's'

Takashimaya (106/A4)
★ Interesting offspring of a Japanese department store; good for special presents. The lower storey houses the *Tea Box*, a good stop for lunch. *Mon-Sat 10.00-18.00, Thurs 10.00-20.00; 693 5th Avenue, between 54th and 55th Street; Subway: 5th Avenue, E, F*

ELECTRONIC GOODS

Adorama (109/F4)
Good value photographic equipment. *42 West 18th Street, between 5th and 6th Avenue; Subway: 18th Street, 1*

CompUSA (110/A1)
This massive hard and software supermarket covers an entire block. On Tuesdays and Sundays the *New York Times* lists the bargains and latest special offers. *420 5th Avenue, between 37th and 38th Street; Tel: 764-6224; Subway: 34th Street, B, D, F, N, Q, R*

J & R Music World (114/B4)
Cameras, video cameras, computers, CDs and more at very reasonable prices. Demonstrations of equipment are given.

23 Park Row/Beekman Street; Subway: City Hall/Brooklyn Bridge, N, R, 4, 5, 6

Software Etc. (110/A4)
Specialists in computer software. On-site software demonstrations are given by experts.
101 5th Avenue/17th Street; Subway: 14th Street/Union Square, 4, 5, 6, L, N, R

Tri-State Camera (109/F3)
Camera and computer bargains; free advice.
650 Avenue of the Americas/20th Street; Subway: 23rd Street, F

FLEA MARKETS

On Sundays, flea markets compete with street fairs and crafts fairs for shoppers. Further information in local magazines.

Annex Antiques Fair & Flea Market (109/F2-3)
Antiques and all kinds of bric-a-brac invite you to come and rummage.
Sat and Sun from 08.00, depending on the weather; 6th Avenue/24th-27th Street; Subway: 23rd Street, F. Next door is the Indoor Antiques Fair with 60 stalls. 122 W 26th Street

I.S. 44 Market (105/D1)
New and second-hand clothes, jewellery and T-shirts.
Sun from 10.00; Columbus Avenue/76th Street; Subway: 72nd Street, B, C

GIFTS & SOUVENIRS

Calvin Klein (106/A3)
Designer clothes and perfumes in futuristic surroundings.

654 Madison Avenue/60th Street; Subway: 59th Street, N, R

Dean & DeLuca (114/B1)
★ ❂ Gourmet shops with a large selection of cookbooks and cooking utensils. The Espresso bar is popular with trendy downtown New Yorkers.
560 Broadway/Prince Street; Subway: Prince Street, R

MOMA Design Store (105/F4)
★ Basic and decorative consumer goods, and reproductions of works from the Museum of Modern Art's collection.
44 West 53rd Street, between 5th and 6th Avenue; Subway: 47th-50th Street, B, D, F, Q

Tiffany & Co. (106/A4)
Legendary department store for jewellery. Worth a browse. Small silver items sold on the 2nd floor.
727 5th Avenue/57th Street; Subway: 57th Street, B, Q

Warner Bros. Studio Store (106/A3)
★ Anything you could possibly imagine, endorsed by Bugs Bunny and his cartoon friends.
1 East 57th Street/5th Avenue; Subway: 57th Street, B, Q

William Sonoma (114/B1)
★ Department store for cooking utensils and regional American ingredients.
580 Broadway, between Houston and Prince Street; Subway: Prince Street, N, R

JEWELLERY

Boregaard (106/A4)
★ Creative designs in the Diamond District. The wedding

rings are particularly beautiful.
*18 East 53rd Street, between 5th
Avenue and Madison Avenue;
Tel: 826-3660; Subway: 47th-50th
Street, B, D, F, Q*

Robert Lee Morris (114/B1)
Jewellery and leather accessories
by this innovative designer.
*400 West Broadway, between Spring
and Broome Street; Subway: Prince
Street, R*

Time Will Tell (106/A1)
Old, valuable wristwatches.
*962 Madison Avenue, between 75th
and 76th Street; Subway: 77th Street, 6*

MALLS

South Street Seaport (114/C4)
Once a port for sailing ships, this
area has now been converted into
a museum complex, complete
with gift and souvenir shops,
boutiques, bookshops and galleries selling arts and crafts.
*Mon-Sat 10.00-21.00, Sun 11.00-
20.00; Pier 17, East River; Subway:
Fulton Street, 2, 3, 4, 5*

World Financial Center (114/A4)
Shops in the atrium selling clothes, CDs, chocolates, etc.
*Mon-Fri 10.00-19.00, Sat/Sun
12.00-17.00; Battery Park City; Subway: World Trade Center, 1, 9, C, E,
N, R*

RECORDS & MUSIC

Bleecker Bob's
Golden Oldies (109/F6)
A large selection of LPs and sin-
gles from the 1950s to the 1970s.
*118 West 3rd Street, between Mac-
Dougal Street and Avenue of the
Americas; Subway: West 4th Street,
A, B, C, D, E, F, Q*

Colony Records (105/E5)
New releases and golden oldies.
Ordering service.
*1619 Broadway/49th Street; Sub-
way: 47th-50th Street, B, D, F, Q*

Gryphon Record Shop (105/D1)
Specializes in rare classical and
jazz records as well as tapes.
More than 90,000 to choose
from.
*233 West 72nd Street, between Bro-
adway and West End Avenue; Subway: 72nd Street, 1, 2, 3, 9*

HMV (105/D1)
Classical, pop and jazz music on
two floors.
*2081 Broadway/72nd Street; Sub-
way: 72nd Street, 1, 2, 3, 9*

Jazz Record Center (109/E2)
Specializes exclusively in jazz
records.
*Tues-Sat; 236 West. 26th Street,
between 7th Avenue and 8th Avenue, 8th floor; Subway: 23rd Street,
A, C, E*

Tower Records
Outstanding selection of music
CDs. Three stores in various lo-
cations, all of them open 24 hours
a day.
*692 Broadway/4th Street; Subway:
Broadway/Lafayette Street, B, D, F,
Q* **(110/B6)**. *1961 Broadway/66th
Street; Subway: 66th Street, 1, 9*
(105/D2)

Virgin Megastore (105/E5)
★ The largest selection of music
and multimedia products and
books you will find anywhere in
the city. There is also a café in the
basement.
*1540 Broadway, between 45th and
46th Street; Subway: Times Square,
1, 2, 3, N, R*

A good night's sleep

There's no shortage of good hotels in Manhattan,
but be sure to book in advance

In a city where real estate prices and labour costs are increasingly high, it is difficult to find comfortable, low-priced accommodation. There are few hotel rooms for less than $90 a night. Hordes of business travellers with expense accounts and well-to-do tourists keep the hotels full. Anyone wishing to stay in Manhattan is advised to reserve accommodation in advance.

Your choice of hotel will no doubt be based on location as well as price. The central theatres, museums and shopping areas are within comfortable walking distance from midtown Manhattan. Staying in this area will save time and money, as you won't have to fork out for bus fares, subway tickets or taxis.

As is common in the USA, overnight prices will be given per room and not per person. Two people staying in a double room often does not cost much more than a single. Hotels that provide breakfast will calculate it separately. A 13.25% state tax as well as a $2 room tax are added to the net price. Double rooms normally contain one double bed, less often two singles. You can express your preference in advance.

Rooms in the hotels listed below should be equipped with at least the following: air-conditioning, en-suite bathroom with hot water, colour television and telephone. More expensive hotels should offer room service, porters, rooms with minibars and an in-house restaurant. Room prices vary according to their size, fittings and location within the building. Many hotels offer special summer and weekend deals or special rates for longer stays (for advance bookings). All-in accommodation and flight packages booked through your travel agent often prove to be better value than making your

The Waldorf-Astoria in the heart of the city, once the most glamorous hotel in New York, still lives up to its name

own arrangements once you are in New York.

If you are making your own travel arrangements, make sure you arrive at your hotel before 6pm, otherwise you may find that your reservation has been cancelled. If you are likely to arrive later, ring the hotel in good time to let them know the approximate time of your arrival. You will normally be required to give them your credit card number in order to secure the booking. A hotel reservation per credit card is counted to be binding if it is not cancelled in time. Rooms should be vacated on the day of departure by midday.

Keep a few dollars in your pocket for tips. Chambermaids are tipped at least $5. For long-term stays in less sophisticated hotels, $1 per night is accept-able, while in the more sophisticated ones, $2 per night is the norm.

Don't leave any valuables in your room, as hotels are neither sufficiently protected against theft, nor able to compensate losses. You can rent safety-deposit boxes at the reception. This is not an absolute guarantee, but it reduces the risk of loss.

In most good hotels, the concierge will help you obtain reservations in booked-out restaurants or arrange for theatre or opera tickets. A tip is customary.

As to the categories: good value accommodation in New York is considered to be anything up to $150 per night. The medium price bracket ranges from $150 to $250, while rooms over $250 are classified as expensive.

MARCO POLO SELECTION: HOTELS

1 Beacon
Not the most comfortable but very reasonably priced (page 68)

2 Beverly
Simple family-owned hotel (page 67)

3 Franklin
Oppulance and style at a good price (page 67)

4 The Inn at Irving Place
Intimate luxury with a down-town location (page 63)

5 The Mark
Excellent service from friendly and welcoming staff (page 63)

6 Milburn
Comfort and value in the Upper West Side (page 67)

7 Paramount
High-tech design in the Theater District (page 67)

8 Wales
A cosy, comfortable Upper East Side hotel (page 68)

9 Washington Square
The best value in downtown New York (page 69)

10 The Wyndham
Excellently located near Central Park (page 68)

GROUP A HOTELS

Top of the range, from $250 per double.

Algonquin (105/F5)
The newly renovated rooms have given a new lease of life to this distinguished hotel, frequented by the literati. Still good: the *Oak Room Bar*. 165 rooms.
59 West 44th Street, between 5th and 6th Avenue; Tel: 840-6800; Fax: 944-1419; Subway: 42nd Street, B, D, F, Q

The Box Tree (106/B5)
Charming old townhouse, renovated with beautiful fabrics and antique furnishings. 13 rooms.
250 East 49th Street, between 2nd and 3rd Avenue; Tel: 758-8320; Fax: 308-3899; Subway: 51st Street, 6

Doral Park Avenue (110/A1)
Completely renovated. Guests have access to the Doral Fitness Center nearby. 188 rooms.
70 Park Avenue/38th Street; Tel: 687 7050; Fax: 779-0148; Subway: Grand Central, 4, 5, 6, 7

Drake Swissôtel (106/A4)
Swiss efficiency and a central location are this hotel's main assets. The *Drake Bar* serves Swiss specialities. 550 rooms.
440 Park Avenue/56th Street; Tel: 421-0900; Fax: 371-4190; Subway: Lexington Avenue, E, F

Elysée (106/A4)
Newly renovated, central location. The in-house *Monkey Bar* is a classy restaurant/bar. 99 rooms.
60 East 54th Street, between Madison and Park Avenue; Tel: 753-1066; Fax: 980-9278; Subway: Fifth Avenue, E, F

Essex House (105/F3)
Tastefully renovated, by Central Park. 593 rooms.
160 Central Park South, between 6th and 7th Avenue; Tel: 247-0300; Fax: 315-1839; Subway: Columbus Circle, 1, 9, A, B, C, D

The Inn at Irving Place (110/B4)
★ Romantic luxury in the 12 suites of a Victorian townhouse. Good bar!
56 Irving Place between 17th and 18th Street; Tel: 533-4600; Fax: 533-4611; Subway: Union Square, L, N, R, 4, 6

Inter-Continental New York (106/A5)
Elegant hotel, perfect for business executives. In-house fitness and massage centres. Free limousine service to Wall Street. 686 rooms.
111 East 48th Street, between Park and Lexington Avenue; Tel: 755-5900; Fax: 644-0079; Subway: 51st Street, 6

The Lowell (106/A3)
Peaceful and personal. The *Pembrooke Room* is a charming restaurant serving exquisite breakfasts and afternoon teas. Mick Jagger and George Michael are among the celebrity guests who have stayed here. 65 rooms (some with open fireplace).
28 East 63rd Street, between Madison and Park Avenue; Tel: 838-1400; Fax: 319-4230; Subway: 59th Street, 4, 5, 6

The Mark (102/A6)
★ Stylishly renovated hotel near the Fifth Avenue museums. All rooms have video recorders. The marble-lined bathrooms are spacious and grand and the service is particularly praiseworthy. The hotel has its own restaurant

(Mark's) and cake shop *(Sant Ambroeus)*. 180 rooms.

25 East 77th Street, between 5th Avenue and Madison Avenue; Tel: 744-4300; Fax: 472-5714; Subway: 77th Street, 6

The Marriott Marquis (105/E5)

◁◈▷ Futuristic, predominantly glass building (even the elevators are transparent). The bar on the 8th floor and the 46th–floor restaurant are revolving and offer fantastic views. 1911 rooms.

1535 Broadway, between 45th and 46th Street; Tel: 398-1900; Fax: 704-8966; Subway: 42nd Street/Times Square, 1, 2, 3, 9, N, R

The Mercer (114/B1)

The second hotel in the SoHo shopping area. Exhibits art and design. 81 rooms.

99 Prince Street, between Mercer and Greene Streets; Tel: 226-5656; Fax: 226-8224; Subway: Prince Street, N, R

Millennium Broadway (105/F5)

◁◈▷ New 52-storey building with a wonderful view of the city. Particularly well suited to business travellers: computer terminals in the rooms provide access to various data networks. 638 rooms.

145 West 44th Street, between 6th Avenue and Broadway; Tel: 768-4400; Fax: 789-7688; Subway: 42nd Street/Times Square, 1, 2, 3, 7, 9, N, R

Morgans (110/A1)

Not content with designing just the interior, Andrée Putman was also responsible for designing the uniforms worn by the excellent staff. Video recorders provided on request. 114 rooms (relatively small). Lively bar.

237 Madison Avenue, between 37th and 38th Street; Tel: 686-0300; Fax: 779-8352; Subway: 33rd Street, 6

The New York Hilton (105/F4)

46-storey skyscraper with 2141 rooms. Guests receive individual service from the staff who, between them, speak approximatly 30 languages.

1335 Avenue of the Americas, between 53rd and 54th Street; Tel: 586-7000; Fax: 315-1374; Subway: 7th Avenue; B, D, E

New York Palace (106/A5)

◁◈▷ A black glass palace with 900 large rooms. Also houses the celebrity restaurant *Le Cirque 2000*.

455 Madison Avenue/50th Street; Tel: 888-7000; Fax: 303-6000; Subway: 51st Street, E, F

Rihga (105/F4)

◁◈▷ Luxury hotel with 492 suites. The upper floors of this 54-storey building offer spectacular views.

151 West 54th Street/7th Avenue; Tel: 307-5000; Fax: 765-6530; Subway: 7th Avenue, B, D, E

The Royalton (105/F5)

High-tech hotel designed by Frenchman Philippe Starck. Futuristic lobby with bar and restaurant '44' 167 rooms.

44 West 44th Street, between 5th and 6th Avenue; Tel: 869-4400; Fax: 869-8965; Subway: 42nd Street, B, D, F, Q

Sheraton Park Avenue (110/A1)

The wood-panelled bar and library give an old English atmosphere. Guests may use nearby fitness club. 151 rooms.

45 Park Avenue/37th Street; Tel: 685-7676; Fax: 889-3139; Subway: 33rd Street, 6

New York's Luxury Hotels

The Carlyle (106/A1)
Victorian decor and discreetly attentive, efficient staff. According to food critic Tim Zagat, it is 'probably the best-run hotel in New York'. 198 rooms; from $350 for a double room.
35 East 76th Street at Madison Avenue; Tel: 744-1600; Fax: 717-4682; Subway: 77th Street, 6

Four Seasons (106/A3)
This relatively new establishment sticks to the old tradition of grandeur and splendour. The restaurants and rooms are spacious and luxurious. The vast modern lobby has been likened by critics to the inside of a pyramid. 367 rooms; from $570 for a double room.
57 East 57th Street, between Madison and Park Avenue; Tel: 758-5700; Fax: 758-5711; Subway: 5th Avenue/ 53rd Street, E, F

The Peninsula (106/A4)
Art-Nouveau furniture and antiques plus superb service. A luxurious fitness club and a pool with a view of the Fifth-Avenue skyscrapers are located in the upper storey. The Pentop Bar is romantic during the summer – it's up on the roof, under the stars. 242 rooms, starting from about $450 for a double room.
700 5th Avenue/55th Street; Tel: 247-2200; Fax: 903-3949; Subway: 5th Avenue, E, F

The Pierre (106/A3)
Old-fashioned luxury with style and excellent service. Many of the rooms offer a view over Central Park, while the Café

Pierre serves up first-class cuisine. 205 rooms; from $395 for a double room.
2 East 61st Street/5th Avenue; Tel: 838-8000; Fax: 758-1615; Subway: 5th Avenue, N, R

The Plaza (106/A3)
Luxuriance in the splendour of one of New York's architectural landmarks. If you can't stretch to the price of a room, just drop in after a long day's sightseeing and relax with a drink or two at the *Oak Bar* or with a bite to eat in the *Oyster Bar*. To see and be seen, you should breakfast or brunch at the *Palm Court*. 800 rooms; from $380 for a double room.
768 5th Avenue/59th Street; Tel: 759-3000; Fax: 546-5324; Subway: 5th Avenue, N, R

Plaza-Athénée (106/A2)
Famous guests such as Elizabeth Taylor stay overnight here in the suite named after them. Elegant. The restaurant *Le Régence* is on the premises.153 rooms; from $370 for a double room.
37 East 64th Street, between Madison and Park Avenue; Tel: 734-9100; Fax: 772-0958; Subway: Lexington Avenue, N R

St. Regis (106/A4)
This old townhouse, dating back to 1904, was once the home of John Jacob Astor. Recently restored to its former glory by the Sheraton chain, it boasts an excellent restaurant – *Lespinasse*. (see page 44). 316 rooms; from $455 for a double.
2 East 55th Street/5th Avenue; Tel: 753-4500; Fax: 787-3447; Subway: 5th Avenue, E, F

Wallow in luxury at the Plaza

Soho Grand Hotel (114/B2)
In the middle of Soho. Most of the (not very large) rooms have a view of the urban landscape. The restaurant *Canal House* and the lively *Grand Bar* are also on the premises. 369 rooms,
310West Broadway/Grand Street; Tel: 965-3000; Fax: 965-3142; Subway: Canal Street, N, R

The Stanhope (102/A6)
◁◃ On Fifth Avenue's museum mile. Many of the rooms and suites (with Louis XVI furniture) offer a pleasant view onto the greenery of Central Park and the Metropolitan Museum. 114 rooms.
995 5th Avenue/81st Street; Tel: 288-58 00; Fax: 517-0088; Subway: 77th Street, 6

United Nations Park Hyatt (106/C5)
Diplomats from UN headquarters stay here. Glass-covered swimming pool on the 27th floor. Indoor hotel tennis court. 427 rooms.
1 UN Plaza, 44th Street/1st Avenue; Tel: 758-1234; Fax: 702-5051; Subway: Grand Central, 4, 5, 6, 7

The Waldorf-Astoria (106/A5)
Luxury hotel that still bears traces of the opulent lifestyle enjoyed by the likes of the Astors, the Vanderbilts and the Kennedys. Rooms in the Waldorf Tower are highly exclusive. 1380 rooms.
301 Park Avenue/50th Street; Tel: 355-3000; Fax: 872-7272; Subway: 51st Street, 6

Westbury (106/A2)

On Madison Avenue's shopping mile. This hotel exudes British charm. The in-house *Polo* restaurant serves good modern American dishes. 235 rooms.
15 East 69th Street/Madison Avenue; Tel: 535-2000; Fax: 535-5058; Subway: 68th Street, 6

GROUP B HOTELS

Medium-priced, between $150 and $250.

Beverly (106/B5)

★ Small, family-run hotel. Simple and clean, the service is more personal than in the larger hotels. It has a pharmacy and a coffee shop. 200 rooms.
125 East 50th Street/Lexington Avenue; Tel: 753-2700; Fax: 715-2452; Subway: 51st Street, 6

Empire Radisson (105/E3)

Opposite Lincoln Center, near Central Park. Boldly furnished in-house restaurant *Merlot* and the *Iridium* jazz club. 372 rooms.
44 West 63rd Street/Broadway; Tel: 265-7400; Fax: 315-0349; Subway: 66th Street, 1, 9

The Franklin (102/B5)

★ Small, newly renovated rooms for $145, including coffee and croissants for breakfast. Ideally situated for visits to the museum mile on Fifth Avenue. 53 rooms.
164 East 87th Street, between Lexington and 3rd Avenue; Tel: 369-1000; Fax: 369-8000; Subway: 86th Street, 4, 5, 6

Gramercy Park (110/B3)

Great location for all downtown activities. View onto the greenery of Gramercy Park. 507 rooms.
2 Lexington Avenue/21st Street; Tel: 475-4320; Fax: 505-0535; Subway: 23rd Street, 6

Lexington (106/B5)

Central location for shopping enthusiasts. 750 rooms.
511 Lexington Avenue/48th Street; Tel: 755-4400; Fax: 751-4091; Subway: 51st Street, 6, E, F

The Mansfield (105/F5)

Renovated, has video recorders and a video library. Breakfast and cappuccino bar are included in price (approx. $195). 122 rooms.
12 West 44th Street, between 5th and 6th Avenue; Tel: 944-6050; Fax: 764-4477; Subway: 42nd Street, B, D, F

Mayflower (105/E3)

Front rooms open onto Central Park; the back rooms look out over the city. Popular with artists. 377 rooms.
15 Central Park West, between 61st and 62nd Street; Tel: 265-0060; Fax: 265-0227; Subway: Columbus Circle, 1, 9, A, B, C, D

Milburn (104/C1)

★ In the best residential area of the Upper West Side. Modern, practical two-room suites with simple cooking facilities. 92 units; studios from $119.
242 West 76th Street, on the corner of West End Avenue; Tel: 362-1006; Fax: 721-5476; Subway: 72nd Street, 1, 2, 3, 9

Paramount (105/E5)

★ Trendy Theater District hotel designed by internationally-acclaimed French designer Philippe Starck. Makes up in style for what it lacks in service, despite being very friendly. Video recorders in each room. In-house coffee shop, the restaurant *Coco Pazzo Teatro*, a fitness room and the bar *Whiskey*. 600 rooms. Rooms from $99, most are around $150.

235 West 46th Street, between Broadway and 8th Avenue; Tel: 764-5500; Fax: 354-5237; Subway: 42nd Street, A, C, E

Pennsylvania (109/E1)

Reputed to be one of the safest hotels in New York City, despite its location (near Pennsylvania Station and Madison Square Garden). 1705 rooms, from $150.

401 7th Avenue, between 32nd and 33rd Street; Tel: 736-5000; Fax: 502-8712; Subway: 34th Street, 1, 2, 3, 9

Salisbury (105/F4)

Good location near Carnegie Hall and Central Park. 205 large rooms.

123 West 57th Street, between 6th and 7th Avenue; Tel: 246-1300; Fax: 977-7752; Subway: 57th Street, N, R

Wales (102/A4)

★ Near the Metropolitan Museum and the delights of Madison Avenue shopping, with 84 small renovated rooms. Hotel restaurant, *Sarabeth*, serves a good breakfast and brunch.

1295 Madison Avenue, between 92nd and 93rd Street; Tel: 876-6000; Fax: 860-7000; Subway: 96th Street, 6

The Wyndham (105/F3)

★ Charming old family-owned hotel. Both the price and the location (between Carnegie Hall, Central Park and Fifth Avenue) make it an excellent choice. 200 rooms.

42 West 58th Street, between 5th and 6th Avenue; Tel: 753-3500; Fax: 754-5638; Subway: 57th Street, N, R

For rooms up to $150 per double.

Beacon (105/D1)

★ Old apartment block hotel on the Upper West Side with meagre, but renovated rooms, some (20th floor upwards) with a view of Central Park. Has its own disco, the *China Club* (best night: Monday). 80 rooms: singles from $110, doubles from $130.

2130 Broadway, between 74th and 75th Street; Tel: 787-1100; Fax: 724-0839; Subway: 72nd Street, 1, 2, 3, 9

Broadway Inn (105/E5)

41 renovated rooms in an old building in the middle of the Theater District. Single rooms from $85, doubles from $105, including breakfast. *264 West 46th Street/8th Ave; Tel: 997-9200; Fax: 768-2807; Subway: Times Square, 1, 2, 3, N, R*

Country Inn the City (101/D6)

Four quiet studios in a private Upper West Side townhouse. Smoking not allowed. $135/145.

West 77th Street between Broadway and Westend Avenue; Tel: 580-4183; Fax: 874-3981; Subway: 79th Street, 1

Day's Hotel Midtown (105/E5)

Renovated hotel in the Theater District, with rooftop swimming pool. 366 rooms.

790 8th Avenue, between 48th and 49th Street; Tel: 581-7000; Fax: 974-0291; Subway: 50th Street, C, E

Excelsior (101/E6)

An established hotel right on Central Park, opposite the Museum of Natural History. 160 rooms, from $139.

45 West 81st Street, between Columbus Avenue and Central Park West;

Tel: 362-9200; Fax: 721-2994; Subway: 81st Street, B, C

Hotel 17   (110/B4)
✠ For young people on short budget (approx. $77/day, $350/week). Small rooms and shared bathrooms. A former homeless shelter.
225 East 17th Street, between 2nd and 3rd Avenue; Tel: 475-2845; Fax: 677-8178; Subway: Union Square, 4, 5, 6, N, R

Olcott   (105/E1)
Near Central Park on the Upper West Side, this hotel is old, but plush and clean. Single rooms from $90. 250 rooms.
27 West 72nd Street, between Central Park West and Columbus Avenue; Tel: 877-4200; Fax: 580-0511; Subway: 72nd Street, B, C

Ramada Milford Plaza   (105/E5)
Pre-war skyscraper with 1300 rooms. Within easy walking distance of all Broadway theatres.
270 West 45th Street/8th Avenue; Tel: 869-3600; Fax: 944-8357; Subway: 50th Street, C, E

Washington Square   (109/F5)
★ Basic but clean hotel in the heart of Greenwich Village. Ask for one of the renovated rooms. Also houses the newly-opened restaurant *C3* with its Mexican-inspired cuisine. 150 rooms.
103 Waverly Place/MacDougal St; Tel: 777-9515; Fax: 979-8373; Subway: West 4th Street, A, B, C, D, E, F, Q

Westpark   (105/E3)
Between the Theater District and Lincoln Center. 85 rooms.
308 West 58th Street, between 8th and 9th Avenue: Tel: 246-6440; Fax: 246-3131; Subway: Columbus Circle, 1, 9, A, B, C, D

BED & BREAKFAST

The steady rise in hotel prices has meant an increase in the number of places offering bed and breakfast. Agencies offer all kinds of accommodation, from separate apartments to rooms in a real New York apartment. Prices start at $70. The quality varies.
City Lights, P.O. Box 20355, New York, NY, 10028; Tel: 737-7049; Fax: 535-2755; and *Urban Ventures, P.O. Box 426, New York, NY 10024; Tel: 594-5650; Fax: 947-9320.*

FOR YOUNG PEOPLE

Vanderbilt YMCA   (106/B5)
Small rooms for one to four people, with television. Soap and handtowels are provided. Central location. 370 beds. Singles cost $53 and rooms for four cost $112.
224 East 47th Street, between 2nd and 3rd Avenue; Tel: 756-9600; Subway: Grand Central, 4, 5, 6, 7

West Side Y   (105/E3)
Good location near Lincoln Center. 525 rooms. Singles: $55, doubles: $65. 525 rooms.
5 West 63rd Street, between Central Park West and Broadway; Tel: 787-4400; Subway: Columbus Circle, 1, 9, A, B, C, D

DISCOUNT RESERVATIONS

These firms buy large numbers of rooms and sell them at considerably cheaper prices:
Hotel Reservations Network; Tel: (214) 361-7311; Fax: 361-7299 and *Quickbook; Tel: (212) 532-1660; Fax: 799-6120*

New York diary

*New York is one big theatre. Street parties, processions,
open-air festivals — endless entertainment
that won't cost you a cent*

As soon as spring is in the air, New Yorkers take to the streets to celebrate. Nearly every weekend between May and October, street parties and festivals are held all over town. Details of these events are published in the weekend supplement of the *New York Times* issued on Fridays.

Central Park is a popular location for all kinds of open-air entertainment, including Shakespeare plays, operas and classical music concerts. Jazz is played on Pier 16, Fulton Street, from the beginning of July to mid-August, there is live music every Friday evening in the Museum of Modern Art Sculpture Garden and, in the last two weeks of August, the Lincoln Center holds its annual 'Out-of-Doors' music festival. And the best news is, all this great entertainment is free.

During the hot and humid summer months of July and August, the streets of Manhattan are taken over by tourists, while those New Yorkers who can afford it escape to the country or to the beaches of Long Island do so. Christmas is a festive time. Luxury department stores and shops such as Tiffany's and Macy's vie with one another for the best window displays. Tiny lights glitter and glow in thousands of trees across the city. An enormous Christmas tree is erected in the Rockefeller Center at the beginning of December, when a traditional tree-lighting ceremony is held.

PUBLIC HOLIDAYS

On the following days, local authorities, post offices, schools, shops and most offices are closed:
1 January *(New Year's Day)*
Last Monday in May *(Memorial Day, commemorating those killed in all American wars)*
4 July *(Independence Day)*
First Monday in September *(Labor Day)*
Last Thursday in November *(Thanksgiving)*
25 December *(Christmas Day)*.
Public services are closed, but most offices are open and many shops hold special sales on these days:

Street party celebrations in true American style

Third Monday in January *(Martin Luther King's Birthday)*
Third Monday in February *(President's Day)*
Second Monday in October *(Columbus Day)*
First Tuesday in November *(Election Day)*
11 November *(Veterans' Day)*.

January
The *Chinese New Year* falls some where between January and March. It is celebrated with a 10-day festival launched with fireworks, and the dance of the paper dragon through the streets of Chinatown. Many Chinese restaurants lay on special New Year buffets.
Subway: Canal Street, 6
Mid-January:
National Boat Show. Sailing and motor boats are exhibited in the impressive glass Javits Convention Center.
11th Avenue/West 35th Street; Tel: 216 2000; Subway: 34th Street, A, C, E
End of January to early February:
Winter Antiques Show.

7th Regiment Armory, Park Avenue and 67th Street; Subway: 68th Street, 6

March
17 March:
St. Patrick's Day, which is celebrated with a big parade. Irish Americans march down Fifth Avenue between 44th and 86th Street.
★ End March to end May:
The biggest circus in the world, *Ringling Bros., Barnum & Bailey*, comes to town. *Madison Square Garden, 8th Avenue, between 31st and 33rd Street; Tel: 465-6741; Subway: 34th Street, A, C, E*

May
★ Third weekend in May:
A chance to sample some exotic foods from all over the world at the *Ninth Avenue International Food Festival. 9th Avenue.*

June
End of June to early July:
JVC Jazz Festival New York. Jazz concerts are held in various concert halls and churches across the city. Tickets can be obtained from the ticket agency Ticketron.

MARCO POLO SELECTION: EVENTS

1 4th of July fireworks
Celebrating Independence Day (page 73)

2 New York Marathon
Great spectacle with lots of flair (page 73)

3 Ninth Avenue International Food Festival
Eat your way around the world (page 72)

4 Ringling Bros. Barnum & Bailey
The largest circus in the world. Not only fun for kids (page 72)

5 San Gennaro Festival
Little Italy celebrates a 10-day annual market festival in honour of Naple's patron saint (page 73)

The *Metropolitan Opera* puts on regular open-air evening concerts in the city parks throughout the month. Entrance is free.
End June:
The annual *Gay and Lesbian Pride Day* parade.

July
★ On 4 July at 9 pm fire-works are let off from boats on the East River to celebrate *Independence Day*. The best place to view them is probably from FDR Drive, which is closed to traffic in the evening between 14th and 50th Street.

August
End August:
US Open *tennis championships* in Flushing Meadow, Queens. The finals are held at the beginning of September.
Subway: Willets Point, 7

September
Beginning September:
The start of the opera season which lasts until mid-May.
The *Steuben Day Parade* is held on one of the last two Saturdays in September. German Americans march down Fifth Avenue in commemoration of the Prussian General Friedrich Wilhelm von Steuben, commander of George Washington's American troops during the War of Independence.
★ Mid to end of September:
The *Feast of San Gennaro*, patron saint of Naples, is an annual market/street festival that takes place in the heart of Little Italy. It begins in mid-September and lasts for 10 days. *Mulberry Street to the south of Houston Street:* food, games and the smallest Ferris wheel in the world.

Subway: Prince Street, N, R
End of September to early October:
New York Film Festival held in the *Museum of Modern Art* and in the *Lincoln Center*.

October
End of October:
The *Fall Antiques Show* is held at the *Pier* and lasts for four days. Over 100 antique dealers from all over the United States gather together to trade their wares.
West 52nd Street and Hudson River; Subway: 50th Street, C, E

November
★ First Sunday in the month: *New York Marathon*. It starts at the *Verrazano Bridge* and the finishing line is in *Central Park*.
Last Thursday in November:
The procession floats and gigantic balloons of the *Thanksgiving Day Parade* wend their way from *Central Park West/77th Street* down to *Macy's department store.*

The New York Marathon: thousands of athletes take part every year

Out on the town

Broadway shows and Shakespeare plays, live jazz and classical concerts, ballet and opera, nightclubs and piano bars — something to suit every mood and pocket

In the world's entertainment capital, nightlife begins as soon as work ends. New Yorkers tend to go out straight from work, without stopping off at home beforehand, meeting up in their favourite bar for a drink or in a restaurant for an early dinner, before going on to the theatre, concert hall or cinema. The huge choice of entertainment on offer is something New Yorkers tend to take for granted, but for the uninitiated it can be overwhelming. One thing's for sure: all tastes and budgets are catered for.

New York boasts some spectacular nightclubs and prides itself on its vibrant club culture. But fashions change so fast that it's difficult to keep up with the 'in' and 'out' places. A nightclub may be packed to the hilt one week and a place not to be seen dead in the next. The New York music scene is still very much alive and, again, there are hundreds of live music venues to choose from. The legendary jazz and blues clubs, less prone to the whims of fashion, attract a dedicated following.

If you find difficulty deciding where to go, the critical reviews and listings in the daily newspapers and weekly magazines, like the *New York Times* and the *New Yorker*, are a good starting point, while a good source of information on the latest clubs and live music venues is the *Village Voice*. *Time Out* also publish a weekly entertainment guide every Wednesday.

BARS

Hotel bars in New York stay open until past midnight and are the perfect places to go for a classic cocktail. Sip a Dry Martini or a Manhattan, a Gimlet or a Whisky Sour, skilfully mixed by the bartender, and soak up the atmosphere. You can also visit one of the many restaurant bars around town for a relaxed evening and a bite to eat at the counter. Otherwise the run-of-the-mill New York bar doesn't differ much from a pub in that it's a

Broadway Theater: formerly The Colony where Walt Disney's first film was shown in 1928, now New York's top venue for musicals

place where most punters come to drink beer and socialize, and the food – basic fare, usually steak or hamburgers – is of secondary importance.

HOTEL BARS

Algonquin (105/F5)
The lounge bar of this hotel, once a favourite haunt for literary figures, is still a popular watering-hole with the intelligentsia.
59 West 44th Street, between 5th and 6th Avenue; Tel: 840-6800; Subway: 42nd Street, B, D, F, Q

Bemelman's Bar (106/A1)
A stylish and romantic piano bar in the Carlyle Hotel.
35 East 76th Street/Madison Avenue; Tel: 744-1600; Subway: 77th Street, 6

The Oak Room Bar (106/A3)
★ Oasis within the Plaza Hotel that serves good cocktails. A nostalgic smoky atmosphere, reminiscent of an old British gentleman's club.
768 5th Avenue/59th Street; Tel: 759-3000; Subway: 5th Avenue, N, R

Pentop Bar (106/A4)
⭐ A glass house 23 stories up on the roof of the Peninsula Hotel. In the summer, you can sit outside on the terrace amid the sky-scrapers.
700 5th Avenue/55th Street; Tel: 247-2200; Subway: 5th Avenue, E, F

The Royalton Bar (105/F5)
The bar area encompasses the whole lobby. High-tech design.
44 West 44th Street, between 5th and 6th Avenue; Tel: 869-8844; Subway: 42nd Street, B, D, F, Q

RESTAURANT BARS

Balthazar (114/B1)
★ Hip restaurant with an equally trendy bar. Very promising.
80 Spring Street/Crosby Street; Tel: 965-1414; Subway: Spring Street, 6

Beauty Bar (110/B4)
Downtowners now frolic in this former beauty salon.
231 East 14th Street; between 2nd Avenue and 3rd Avenue; Tel: 539-1389; Subway: 14th Street, L, N, R, 4, 6

Bowery Bar (110/B6)
A converted garage, popular with celebrities and models. *Très* New York – you have to dress 'hip' if you want to get in. The food is forgettable, but the bar is really buzzing.
358 Bowery/East 4th Street; Tel: 475-2220; Subway: Astor Place, 6

The Bubble Lounge (114/B2)
One drinks champagne here, amid comfortable plush furniture. *228 West Broadway/White Street; Tel: 431-3433; Subway: Franklin Street, 1, 9*

Mickey Mantle's (105/F3)
TV and drinks for baseball fans.
42 Central Park South, between 5th and 6th Avenue; Tel: 688-7777; Subway: Columbus Circle, 1, 9, A, B, C, D

P.J. Clarke's (106/B4)
The tradition is Irish, but the atmosphere is very New York. A single's meeting place with nostalgic flair.
915 3rd Avenue/55th Street; Tel: 759-1650; Subway: Lexington/3rd Avenue, E, F

Pravda (114/B1)
Equally great roles are played by vodka and the models' fashions present here. *281 Lafayette Street/ Prince Street; Tel: 226-4696; Subway: Prince Street, N, R*

South Street Seaport (114/C4)
↘↗ ☂ ☃ On mild summer evenings, bright young Wall Street brokers gather outside the cafés and restaurants on Pier 17 to wind down after the day's frantic dealing.
Subway: Fulton Street, 2, 3, 4, 5

Temple Bar (110/B6)
★ Old-fashioned bar. The menu is limited, but it's a good place for a late-night drink. Unlike most other bars, there are no restricted areas for smokers.
332 Lafayette Street/Bleecker Street; Tel: 925-4242; Subway: Broadway-Lafayette Street, B, D, F, Q

I Tre Merli (114/B1)
If you're doing the tour of the SoHo galleries, this is a good place to stop off for a break and a glass of quality wine: the proprietor is a wine-grower.
463 West Broadway, between Houston and Prince Street; Tel: 254-8699; Subway: Prince Street, R

The 21 Club (105/F4)
Former jockey club decorated with toys dangling from the ceiling. One of the most popular singles bars in the city.
21 West 52nd Street, between 5th and 6th Avenue; Tel: 582-7200; Subway: 47th-50th Street, B, D, F, Q

The following restaurant bars are also worth a visit for a drink and bite to eat:
The *Rainbow Promenade* in the *Rainbow Room* and *The River Café* (for addresses see pp. 45 and 47).

MARCO POLO SELECTION: NIGHT–TIME ENTERTAINMENT

1 Avery Fisher Hall
Home to the New York Philharmonic (page 80)

2 Balthazar
Here one sees and is seen (page 76)

3 The Blue Note
Jazz club featuring celebrity musicians (page 83)

4 Brooklyn Academy of Music
World class productions featuring big international names (page 78)

5 City Center
Often rousing ballet performances (page 80)

6 Joseph Papp Public Theatre
A remarkable repertory theatre (page 78)

7 Knitting Factory
Free jazz and rock in new opend spaces (page 83)

8 Metropolitan Opera
The world's best opera experience (page 80)

9 The Oak Room Bar
Oasis in the Plaza (page 76)

10 S.O.B.'s
For Latin- and reggae- lovers alike (page 82)

Theatre is still *the* number one tourist attraction in New York, over and above the Statue of Liberty and the Empire State Building. There are a total of 250 theatres in the Big Apple. Eight million tickets are sold annually, the majority of which are for the immensely popular Broadway musicals.

The Broadway theatres are all located in and around the Theater District. Big names draw big audiences: like Oscar-winner Julie Andrews in the stage adaptation of *Victor/Victoria* or Hollywood comedians such as Jerry Lewis in the musical *Damn Yankees.* Many plays enjoy exceptionally long runs (*A Chorus Line* ran for 15 years), especially the classic Broadway song and dance shows such as *Beauty and the Beast, Grease!, Masterclass* and *Sunset Boulevard.* There is also a trend towards importing plays and musicals from London: *Cats, Phantom of the Opera* and *Aspects of Love* all enjoyed huge success.

If you want to know the critics' opinions before deciding what to go and see, consult the reviews in the *New York Times* on Fridays and Sundays, and in the *New York Magazine* or the *New Yorker.*

Matinée performances are often given on Wednesdays, Saturdays and Sundays – an alternative for tourists who are unable to procure tickets at the last minute for the popular evening performances. Bear in mind that most theatres are closed on Mondays.
Subway stations in Theater District: 42nd Street and 6th, 7th or 8th Avenue, 49th/50th Street respectively.

Apart from the three main venues – the Vivian Beaumont Theatre in Lincoln Center, the Public Theater and the Brooklyn Academy of Music – there are a number of smaller and cheaper theatres worth checking out.

Blue Man Group (110/B5)
A show that takes the art scene for a ride, with the help of the audience. *Astor Place Theatre, 343 Lafayette Street/Astor Place; Tel: 254-4370; Subway: Astor Place, 6*

Brooklyn Academy of Music (BAM) (O)
★ Hosts plays, dance shows and concerts. Philip Glass, Mark Morris, Robert Wilson, Laurie Anderson and Martha Clarke have all staged productions here. *30 Lafayette Avenue, between St. Felix and Ashland Place, Brooklyn; Tel: 636-4100; Subway: Atlantic Avenue, 2, 3, 4, 5, D, M, Q*

Circle in the Square (105/E5)
This classic off-Broadway theatre stages more obscure and often less accessible plays that would not necessarily draw a wide enough audience to fill the larger, more traditional theatres. *1633 Broadway/50th Street; Tel: 307-2700; Subway: 50th Street, C, E*

Joseph Papp Public Theatre (110/B5)
★ A six-theatre complex where e.g. contemporary Shakespeare adaptations are performed. William Hurt and Al Pacino have starred here. The Public Cinema runs an art film and a retro programme. *425 Lafayette Street/Astor Place; Tel: 539-8500; Subway: Astor Place, 6*

The Kitchen (109/D3)
Important centre for performance art, dance and video.
512 West 19th Street, between 10th and 11th Avenue; Tel: 255-5793; Subway: 18th Street, 1, 9

Manhattan Theater Club (105/F4)
Where ambitious new talents put their acting skills to the test. Arthur Miller's daughter, Rebecca, first trod the boards here.
City Center, 131 West 55th Street, between 6th and 7th Avenue; Tel: 581-1212; Subway: 57th Street, N, R

OPERA/BALLET

New York City has two great opera houses – the Metropolitan Opera and the New York City Opera. The 'Met' is one of the world's most legendary classic operatic venues. It is the ambition of all great opera singers, from Luciano Pavarotti to Placido Domingo, from Kiri Te Kanawa to Jessye Norman, to perform on the Lincoln Center stage. The New York City Opera has a more popular repertoire with a strong American bias. It has been restored to its former splendour under the artistic direction of erstwhile soprano Beverly Sills, and features up-and-coming American operatic stars.

There is a similar rivalry in the world of ballet: the prominent American Ballet Theater (ABT), which puts on classical ballets, such as *Swan Lake*, at the Met, versus the New York City Ballet company, was set up in the 1940s by the renowned choreographer George Balanchine. The New York City Ballet, like the New York City Opera, promotes younger and lesser-known artists. Other New York dance companies perform once or twice a year for a period of several weeks, mainly at the City Center or at the Joyce Theater. The best-known troupes are the Dance Theater of Harlem, the Feld Ballet, the Dance Company of Martha Graham – the late *grande dame* of contemporary dance – Paul Taylor, Alvin Ailey and Merce Cunningham.

The Met by night

City Center (105/F4)
★ *131 West 55th Street, between 6th and 7th Avenue; Tel: 581-7907; Subway: 57th Street, N, R*

Joyce Theater
(Feld Ballet) (109/E3)
175 8th Avenue/19th Street; Tel: 242-0800; Subway: 18th Street, 1, 9

Metropolitan Opera (105/D3)
★ Metropolitan Opera and American Ballet Theater.
Lincoln Center, Broadway/62nd Street; Tel: 362-6000; Subway: 66th Street, 1, 9

New York State Theater (105/D3)
New York City Opera and New York City Ballet.
Lincoln Center, Broadway/62nd Street; Tel: 870-5570; Subway: 66th Street, 1, 9

CONCERTS

The New York Philharmonic, conducted by Kurt Masur, has been playing at the Avery Fisher Hall in Lincoln Center since 1991. Alice Tully Hall is the venue for the Lincoln Center Chamber Music Society, gifted students from the Julliard School of Music and a variety of celebrity guest performers. New York's second largest concert hall (2760 seats) is Carnegie Hall. Its acoustics are widely acclaimed and it is frequently used for recordings.

New York wouldn't be New York without its summertime open-air performances. 'Mostly Mozart' and 'Classical Jazz' are a series of concerts held in the inner courtyard of Lincoln Center. The Metropolitan Opera and the New York Philharmonic give concerts in public parks, four of which are held in Central Park. It's customary to take a picnic with you, including candles and a blanket. The concerts begin in the evening, but if you arrive later than 16.00, you'll have a struggle finding a space on the concert meadow.
Dates and times: Lincoln Center, Tel: 546-2656; City Parks Events Hotline, Tel: 360-3456

Avery Fisher Hall (105/D2)
★ *Lincoln Center, Broadway/62nd Street; Tel: 875-5030; Subway: 66th Street, 1, 9*

Barge Music (115/E4)
♫ Chamber music on a barge with a view of Manhattan.
Sun 16.00, Thurs 19.30; Fulton Ferry Landing, Brooklyn; Tel: (718) 624-4061; Subway: Clark Street, 2, 3 (15-minute walk)

Carnegie Hall (105/E4)
57th Street at 7th Avenue; Tel: 247-7800; Subway: 57th Street, N, R

CINEMAS

More world film premières are shown in New York than anywhere else. They are usually glittering star-studded events.

The latest Hollywood films often run simultaneously in the major première cinemas, but many multiplex cinemas show re-runs and film classics alongside box-office hits. You'll see two queues in front of cinemas: one for ticket holders and one for people waiting to purchase tickets.

The *New York Times* and the *New York Post* provide detailed cinema listings, as do the weekly *New York Magazine* and *The New Yorker*.

NIGHTCLUBS, POP & ROCK

Nothing is more transitory than the reputation of a New York disco or club. Studio 54, Xenon and Area have passed into the history of nightclub legends. It's difficult to say which nightclubs will be around next year and which of those will still be in vogue. A good way of getting to know the scene is to read Michael Musto's gossip column in the *Village Voice*. The latest trend: certain nightclubs are 'in' only on certain nights in the week.

Door policies are often strict and New York bouncers exercise a lot of power. If you're in casual tourist gear, don't expect to get in. If you get turned away from one club, perservere and try a few more. The bouncers' tastes and temperaments vary greatly.

For up-to-date information on live music, refer to *The New Yorker* or the C section of the *New York Times* on Fridays. Most places require a cover charge (CC), which can range from $5 to $50, depending on the weekday and the profile of the musicians and bands playing.

Le Bar Bat   (105/E4)
Tuck into a plate of charcoal-grilled food while listening to live jazz, or dance to some good old rock-n'-roll. Unusual but typically New York.
Su closed CC $10-$20 (from 21.00); 311 West 57th Street, between 8th and 9th Avenue; Tel: 307-7228; Subway: 57th Street, N, R

The Bottom Line   (110/A6)
Debut venue for budding musicians. Stevie Wonder and Bruce Springsteen played here.
CC $15-$20; no credit cards; 15 West 4th Street/Mercer Street; Tel: 228-6300; Subway: West 4th Street, A, B, C, D, E, F, Q

Carbon   (104/C4)
⚡ Huge disco, rooftop terrace with a fantastic view.
CC $25; 605 West 55th Street, between 11th and 12th Avenue; Tel: 582-8282; Subway: Columbus Circle, A, B, C, D, 1, 9

CBGB   (110/B6)
American punk rock was born here. Still a popular SoHo haunt.
CC $3-$10; 315 Bowery/Bleecker Street; Tel: 982-4052; Subway: Astor Place, 6

Hard Rock Café   (105/E4)
♟ Half restaurant (good hamburgers), half teenage disco, decked out with paraphernalia from the history of rock.
221 West 57th Street, between 7th Avenue and Broadway; Tel: 459-9320; Subway: 57th Street, N, R

Mercury Lounge   (110/C6)
Hip! Many a big name got started here. Rock and country music.
CC $6-$15; 217 East Houston Street/ Essex Street; Tel: 260-4700; Subway: 2nd Avenue Station, F

Nell's   (109/E4)
Nightclub on two floors with live jazz upstairs and a disco downstairs. Theme nights.
CC $10-$15; 246 West 14th Street, between 7th and 8th Avenue; Tel: 675-1567; Subway: 14th Street, A, C, E

Rainbow and Stars   (105/F5)
An *art deco* interior, adorned with the vocal artistry of 'classics' like Rosemary Clooney.

CC $40 admission plus dinner; 30 Rockefeller Plaza, 65th floor; Tel: 632-5000; Subway: 47th-50th Street, B, D, F

Roxy (109/D4)

A huge disco with a gigantic roller-skating and roller-blading track.

Tues, Wed (roller-skating), Fri, Sat (dancing); CC $12-$20; 515 West 18th Street, between 10th and 11th Avenue; Tel: 645-5156; Subway: 18th Street, 1, 9

S.O.B.'s (114/A1)

★ For those who love to groove to Brazilian music (Saturdays), Tango (Sundays), Salsa (Mondays) and reggae rhythms

CC $10-$25; 204 Varick Street/ Houston Street; Tel: 243-4940; Subway: Houston Street, 1, 9

Tatou (106/B5)

Dining clubs are enjoying a comeback. Listen to fresh young talent (Mondays) and live jazz while dining on Franco-American cuisine.

New York's legendary jazz club

Classic cocktails

Collins:	Lemon or lime juice, spirits (gin, rum, whisky or brandy), sugar and soda water.
Coolers:	Long, cool drink usually made with wine, port or sherry mixed with lemon, sugar and soda water and served on ice.
Highballs:	Spirits mixed with soda water, ginger beer or cola, on ice.
Juleps:	Long spirit-based drink with fresh mint, sugar and angostura bitters, on ice.
Sours:	Spirits (usually whisky) shaken with lemon or lime juice and sugar.

CC $15-$20; 151 East 50th Street, between 3rd and Lexington Avenue; Tel: 753-1144; Subway: 51st Street, 6

Wetlands (114/A2)
Loud, shrill, young and live every night – from funk to folk plus pop and psychedelic. For those with steady nerves and hard-working ear drums the Wetlands is definitely worth a visit.
CC $5-$12; 161 Hudson Street/ Laight Street; Tel: 966-4225; Subway: Canal Street, 1, 9, A, C, E

JAZZ/BLUES

The Blue Note (109/F6)
★ The legendary club plays host to some of the biggest names in jazz. Booking essential.
C C: $25-$50; 131 West 3rd Street at 6th Avenue; Tel: 475-8592; Subway: West 4th Street, A, B, C, D, E, F, Q

Knickerbocker Bar & Grill (110/A5)
Wood-panelled bar with excellent pianists (Wednesday to Sunday only).
CC $3.75; 33 University Place/ 9th Street; Tel: 228-8490; Subway: Astor Place, 6

Knitting Factory (114/B3)
★ Recently transferred to more spacious premises: interesting blend of jazz and blues, rock and classical.
CC $8-$15; 74 Leonard Street, between Broadway and Church Street; Tel: 219-3055; Subway: Canal Street, 1, 9, N, R

Manny's Car Wash (102/B5)
Blues and drinks in an authentic laid-back atmosphere.
CC $3-$10; 1558 3rd Avenue, between 87th and 88th Street; Tel: 369-2583; Subway: 86th Street; 4, 5, 6

Sweet Basil (109/F6)
Excellent club — live music from trad jazz to swing to fusion. Has played host to some of the big names in jazz. Dining too.
CC $17.50-$30; 88 7th Avenue/ Bleecker Street; Tel: 242-1785; Subway: Christopher Street, 1, 9

The Village Vanguard (109/E5)
A sophisticated club with first-rate performers.
CC $15; drinks at least $10; no credit cards; 178 7th Avenue South/11th Street; Tel: 255 4037; Subway: 14th Street, 1, 2, 3, 9

Exploring the city by foot

These walking tours are marked in green on the map outside back flap and in the street atlas beginning on page 100

① NEW WORLDS

Exoticism on a small scale and contemporary art: SoHo, Little Italy, Chinatown and East Village (six hours).

The starting point for the walk downtown is *Washington Square Park (p. 24)* with its triumphal arch, which is a meeting place for the students from nearby *New York University (NYU)*, built on a site that was still used as a cemetery in the 18th century. From the south side of the Park, *Thompson Street* points towards the twin towers of the *World Trade Center (p. 29)*. Cross *Bleecker Street*, a mecca for folk musicians in the 1960s and now a magnet for young people, with its street cafés. The route then leads along *West Houston Street* into one of the city's most charming districts: *SoHo (p. 21)* with its cast-iron buildings erected originally as multi-storey factories, shops and warehouses. What they have in common are their cast-iron façade elements and cantilevered ceilings. The area was discovered in the 1960s by artists and students and the buildings were converted into huge loft apartments. One of the typical results of the changing times is to be found on *West Broadway*, at *No. 420* for example, where three of the most famous *galleries* in Manhattan have their premises: *Castelli (p. 54)*, *Sonnabend (p. 54)* and *Cowles*. Strolling through the district with its narrow streets, small boutiques, attractive restaurants and cafés along *Spring Street*, you will come across *Greene Street*, which, with its cobbles and fire escapes, is an impressive left-over of a city that has been glossed over elsewhere. *Broadway* offers further attractions: the *Guggenheim Museum*, *SoHo (p. 36, No. 575)* and *Dean & DeLuca's deli store (p. 58, No. 560)*, with its lively espresso bar. Further along Spring Street, you can follow in the tracks of the New York glitterati of today. A tip for all those who want to catch a glimpse of film stars and models: try the *Bistro Balthazar (No. 80)*. As soon as you reach *Mulberry Street*, you get the feeling you're not in New York any more: the brick houses are only five storeys high, and there's not a skyscraper in sight.

This is the main street in *Little Italy (p. 21)*, a friendly jumble of Italian restaurants with a touch of the cosa nostra. But it's not just the mafia that's disappearing here; Little Italy itself is also struggling for its survival. *Chinatown (p. 19)*, which originally only went as far as *Canal Street (p. 30)*, is spreading northwards. Canal Street itself, running from east to west, is still the centre for all the major Chinese fish, meat and vegetable traders. If you're too timid to venture into one of the many restaurants or the huge supermarket *Kam Man Food Inc. (No. 200)*, why not try a few samples from the mobile traders. To the left of the *Bowery*, the Asian influence starts to fade. And as soon as you cross *Grand Street* to reach *Orchard Street*, you enter another exotic atmosphere: that of the Jewish tailors, with their bargains and special offers. And this world of contrasts does not stop as you go north of *Houston Street* – new ones are added: *Avenue A* and *Tompkins Square Park* in the heart of *East Village (p. 19)* were the stronghold of the hippies in the 1960s and the punk rockers in the 1970s. Nowadays, many artists live here, decked out in T-shirts from *Alphabets (115 Ave. A)*. The general mood is Russian-Ukrainian, something that can actually be tasted in the *Coffee Shop Odessa (119 Ave. A)*, where you can try *Blintzes* – small pancakes filled with cream cheese. On the way to *St. Mark's Place (8th Street; p. 31)*, you'll meet the inhabitants of East Village, with their pink or orange coloured hair and their relaxed lifestyles.

② MONEY RULES THE WORLD

Amongst the money-brokers of Manhattan: a tour around the south tip of Manhattan, where you'll find three of the greatest symbols of New York – the World Trade Center, the Statue of Liberty and the Brooklyn Bridge (six hours).

City Hall (p. 25), New York's town hall located between *Park Row* and *Broadway* and built from 1760-1830, has long become too small to house the city's administration. However, there's still enough room for the Mayor's offices. It faces the *Woolworth Building (Broadway between Barclay Street and Park Place)*, with its copper dome, the proud skyscraper which with a height of 241 m (795ft)was the world's tallest building when it was built in 1913. The district at the *south tip of Manhattan* contains many historic buildings, such as *St. Paul's Chapel*, Manhattan's only church from the Colonial era. Outside, the area buzzes with the hustle and bustle of the business world of financiers and stockbrokers, and the staff in the head offices of shipping companies, trading concerns and lawyers' offices. 50,000 people work in the two towers of the *World Trade Center (p. 29)* alone. Walking from *Broadway*, *Liberty Street* leads to the *South Tower*, where the lift takes visitors to the 107th floor in 58 seconds. From the *viewing platform* on the 110th floor *(closed in strong winds and bad weather)*, the view stretches out over Manhattan. Back on terra firma, our walk leads through the *U.S. Customs Building (at the north-west end of Cortland Square)* and a covered bridge across *West Street* into the *Winter Garden* of the *World Financial Center (p. 17)*. In this glass-domed building, it is possible to eat out under (real) palm trees in any weather conditions (*Coco Pazzo Marina*, would be a good example), to go shopping or take a stroll. The atrium building is a part of *Battery Park City*, a complex that was built in the 1970s and 1980s on the banks of the Hudson river. It was costucted on the building rubble left from the World Trade Center. It is best viewed from a walk along the river bank, past the *North Cove Yacht Harbor*, the departure point for quiet trips down the river. The view from the tree-lined promenade towards the south is just as charming, and from here you can fit the *Statue of Liberty (p. 16)*, *Ellis Island* and *Verrazano Bridge* all onto one photograph in one panoramic view. Further south, past *South Cove* and the *Japanese Ornamental Garden*, the mood becomes sombre, as one approaches the recently erected *Holocaust Museum* in the *Robert Wagner Jr. Memorial Park*. Only a stone's throw away is *Castle Clinton*, where large numbers of immigrants to the New World were processed, until 1860, and where you can now buy tickets for the trip to *Ellis Island (p. 25)*, which was the transition station for immigrants from 1860 on. Another ferry travels from here to *Liberty Island*, where New York's most famous monument lifts her torch high in the air. There are alternatives too – such as a walk through *Battery Park*, where a small *flea market* has emerged, to the *Alexander Hamilton Customs House* on the Bowling Green. The superb *National Museum of the American Indian (p. 39)* has been housed in the former customs building. On Broadway, walk northwards past the old *Trinity Church (p. 16)*, squeezed between the skyscrapers. In the second half of the 19th century, the church used to be the tallest building in Manhattan 80 m (264ft). Opposite is the start of *Wall Street (p. 22)*, a synonym for the hectic goings on in the capital of international finance. On *Broad Street* lies the entrance to the *New York Stock Exchange (p. 26)*, where the famous Dow Jones Index is calculated. A tour around is well worth while. At the intersection between *Broad Street* and *Pearl Street*, you'll find *Fraunces Tavern (p. 26)*, which has been a hostelry for years. Walk along *Water Street*, one of the main streets in the 19th century, now lined by bars and brothels, and *Fulton Street* until you reach *South Street Seaport (p. 59)*, a shopping mall where Wall Street Bankers meet for a drink after work. If you don't want to linger here, take the entrance to the *Brooklyn Bridge (p. 14)* on *Park Row*. On the suspension bridge built in 1883, then regarded as the eighth wonder of the world, pedestrians have their own walkway, slightly raised above the road traffic in the middle of the giant steel structure. The walk is particularly worthwhile at twilight, when the light catches the glass façades of the skyscrapers.

③ THE BETTER PART OF THE BEST

Culture, money and taste – and an excursion to Central Park, where New York shows its best side (six hours).

Prometheus rises in the centre of Manhattan, in the midst of a huge office and shopping complex which a quarter of a million people frequent every day. The Centre does not bear the name of the Greek Titan, but that of its multimillionaire builder *John D. Rockefeller*, who commissioned these 14 buildings *(p. 15)* between 48th and 51st Street and Fifth and Sixth Avenue in 1929. The golden sculpture is one of the decorative sights in the shadow of the *GE Building*. Many streets lead into the skyscraper jungle of Midtown Manhattan. The best way to approach it is to come from the north, making a detour to the venerable department store of *Saks Fifth Avenue (p. 57, 611 5th Avenue)* with its huge toiletries department. This will get you in the mood for the major international names that line New York's most famous boulevard: couturiers such as *Versace (No. 647)*, *Cartier (No. 653)*; stores like *Takashimaya (p. 57, No. 693)*, *Henri Bendel (p. 57, No. 712)* and brand-name producers such as *Coca-Cola (No. 711)*. On *55th Street*, turn right, past the *St. Regis hotel*, and wander along Madison Avenue northwards – through the lobby of the *Sony Building (p. 29)*, where the electronics group has its own museum *(Sony Wonderlab)*. Commerce and Culture again meet a few houses further – in *Niketown USA (p. 56; 6 East 57th Street)*, the flagship store of the famous sports shoe manufacturer. Right next door, at the corner of Fifth Avenue, is the famous jeweller *Tiffany (p. 58)*. The silver department on the second floor has plenty to suit the smaller purse. Visit the *Bergdorf Goodman* department store *(p. 56; 754 Fifth Ave)*, the toyshop *F.A.O. Schwarz (p. 55; 767 Fifth Ave)* and *The Plaza hotel (p. 65; 768 Fifth Ave)*, where you can at least get the feel of the place by walking through the ground floor. You can recover from all the hustle and bustle afterwards by taking a trip into *Central Park (p. 23)*. The route runs in the direction of *72nd Street West*, where Yoko Ono had a garden laid out in front of *The Dakota (p. 30)* in memory of John Lennon – 'Strawberry Fields' *(p. 30)*. Cross right through the Park to Upper Fifth Avenue, where the city's most luxurious apartments and some of the world's most interesting museums are located, such as the *Frick Collection (p. 36; corner of 70th Street)*, concealed in an elegant turn-of-the-century townhouse. *Madison Avenue* shows itself at its finest here, with boutiques owned by European and American designers such as *Ralph Lauren (p. 56; corner of 72nd Street)*. It's best to return to *Fifth Avenue* at *80th Street* at the latest, where the *Metropolitan Museum of Art (p. 37; 1000 Fifth Avenue)*, with its famous massive open staircase, can be seen, along with the *Guggenheim Museum (p. 36; 1071 Fifth Avenue)*, the popular building designed by American architect Frank Lloyd Wright in 1959.

Practical information

Useful addresses and indispensable tips

AMERICAN ENGLISH

In North America, certain terms and usages deviate from British usage. Some of the more frequently encountered examples are: *gas* for *petrol*, *trunk* for *boot*, *car rental* for *car hire*, *toll-free numbers* for *freephone numbers*, *wait staff* for *waiting staff* (in restaurants etc.). In case of doubt you should consult a dictionary.

CONSULATES

Consulate General of Australia
636 5th Avenue
Tel: 245-4000

Consulate General of Britain
845 3rd Avenue
Tel: 752-8400

Consulate General of Canada
1251 Avenue of the Americas
(at 50th Street)
Tel: 596-1600

A bird's eye view of the Queensboro Bridge from the Roosevelt Island tram

Consulate General of Ireland
345 Park Avenue
(at 53rd Street)
Tel: 319-2552

CULTURAL INFORMATION

Information on cultural events can be found in the 'C' section of the *New York Times* on Fridays and in the 'Arts and Leisure' section of the *New York Times* on Sundays. Concise cinema listings are printed every day in the *New York Times*, *New York Post* and *Daily News*. Comprehensive listings for films, plays, concerts, sporting events, etc. are published every Monday in the 'Other Events' column of *New York Magazine*. The weekly *New Yorker* reviews jazz and other musical performances, as well as films, gallery exhibitions, plays, etc. The *Village Voice* and *Time Out* (every Wednesday) are good sources of information on musical events and nightclubs.

CUSTOMS

Each adult is allowed to bring in 200 cigarettes or 50 cigars or 2 kg of tobacco, as well as gifts worth up to $100 each and 1.1 litres of spirits free of duty. It is strictly forbidden to bring in plants, meat, fruit and other fresh products.

ELECTRICITY

110 volts/60 hertz. Many small appliances (hairdryers, electric razors) can function at this low voltage. Adapters for plugs can be bought at: *Radio Shack (several branches, including 42nd Street/6th Avenue; Tel: 944-2540)*

EMERGENCIES

The emergency number to dial for police, fire and ambulance is **911** (free from any call box.)

Hospital Emergency Rooms are obliged by law to treat all patients, even those who are not covered by an American health insurance (e.g. Blue Cross, Blue Shield or Medicaid). All medical bills must be paid, however, immediately on completion of treatment. Most hospitals accept Mastercard and Visa. The cost of medical treatment in America is high, so it's advisable to take out a short-term health insurance (most travel agents will arrange this for you).

INTERNET ADDRESSES

No other city is as crazy about online as New York, nor does any other city offer so much information via the Internet. Offerings extend from the hotel reservation service for the Convention and Visitor Center (www.nycvisit.com) to information on jazz clubs, museums and ticket offices. New York City Reference (www.panix.

com/clay/nyc) presents the best overview.

LOST PROPERTY

There are no municipal lost property offices, but stations, airports and public administration services usually have their own 'Lost and Found' offices. If you've left something behind in a taxi, you should contact the Taxi and Limousine Commission *(Tel: 302-8294)*. It helps if you label your belongings (with an American address). Thieves often throw empty wallets into litter bins. If they are found, the Post Office will forward them anywhere within the USA.

MONEY

1 dollar = 100 cents. Bills come in denominations of $1 (a buck), $2, $5, $10, $20 and $100. Coins come in pieces of 1 (penny), 5 (nickel), 10 (dime), 25 (quarter) and 50 cents. The most common method of payment is by credit card (American Express, Eurocard/Mastercard, Visa). American Express Travellers' Checks are widely accepted, but Eurocheques are not. All banks will cash travellers' cheques and pay cash advances to credit-card holders. Make sure you have some loose change on you when you first arrive, to pay porters, taxi drivers or bus fares, etc.

Foreign currency can be exchanged at a number of banks *(opening hours: Mon-Fri, 09.00-15.00)*, branches of Chemical Bank for example, or at agencies such as *Thomas Cook Currency Service, 511 Madison Avenue/53rd Street (Mon-Fri, 09.00-17.00).*

It is advisable not to ask for your money in large bills ($50 and $100), as they will often be refused, especially by taxi drivers.

POST

The *General Post Office (8th Avenue/33rd Street)* is the only post office open 24 hours a day, every day. Other post offices are open Mon–Sat from *09.00* to *18.00*. Stamps can be bought from the dispensers installed in front of or inside post offices, as well as from pharmacies. A 20g airmail letter to Europe costs 60c, and an airmail postcard costs 50c. New York letter boxes are painted blue.

TELEGRAMS

Telegrams can be ordered by telephone: *Western Union; Tel: 1 (800) 325-6000.* The charges are either paid by credit card or by the subscriber of the telephone line from which you are calling.

TELEPHONES

The telephone system in the States is based on automatic dialling. The Operator (dial 0) can arrange for reverse-charge calls or collect calls (only within the USA) and for telephone calls using American telephone credit cards. The minimum cost of a call in a public telephone box is 25c. Calling from a hotel is much more costly. They can charge up to $1 per unit. Charges for telephoning Europe from a private line (first minute/subsequent minutes): 07.00-13.00: $1.77/1.09; 13.00-18.00: $1.42/0.82; 18.00-07.00: $1.15/0.65. The prefix for Manhattan and the Bronx is 212.

For Brooklyn, Queens and Staten Island, it is 718. The number for directory enquiries for Manhattan and the Bronx (free of charge) is 411. For Brooklyn, Queens and Staten Island: (718) 555-1212. Calls made within the States require the prefix '1' before the area code.

For calls to the States from abroad you will need to dial 001 before the area code and subscriber number. If you're phoning abroad from the States, dial 011 followed by the country code – Australia: 61, Canada: 1, Ireland: 353, United Kingdom: 44 – then the area code omitting the first 0 and finally the subscriber number.

It is possible in many countries to buy a telecom card that you can take with you, to which all your calls can be charged. Contact your national post and telecommunications office for information.

If you have a credit card, you can order a telephone card at the local rate via AT&T (ask for 'Calling Card Service') which can be used in any telephone booth in the country. Newspaper-stands sell telephone cards, with which one can phone by using certain access codes (there are no card telephones as such).

TELEVISION & RADIO

If you're connected to cable, you can switch to 80 TV channels in New York. The major channels you should be able to get in most hotels are ABC (Channel 7), CBS (Channel 2) and NBC (Channel 4), which are broadcast from coast to coast; CNN – Cable News Network (24-hour news), ESPN (24-hour sport), MTV and

VH-1 (24-hour pop videos) and Public Television (Channel 13), which shows documentaries, plays and opera. The bigger networks schedule the day's viewing as follows: 07.00-09.00 breakfast television, 09.00-17.00 daytime TV (stay-at-home parents being the target audience) and from 20.00 onwards, serials and films.

There are about 20 music stations broadcast on FM that cater for all tastes: Classical (96.3), Jazz (101.9), Easy Listening (106.7), Oldies (101.1) New Rock (92.3) and a variety of pop stations. Cultural and news programmes are broadcast on medium wave (AM).

It is possible to get theatre tickets directly from the box office on the night, but performances are often sold out far in advance. This applies not only to the popular Broadway shows, but also to the numerous Off-Broadway and Off-Off-Broadway theatres.

You can order your tickets by phone through one of these services: *Telecharge (Tel: 239-6200)* and *Ticketmaster (Tel: 307-7171).* They will usually add a $5 service charge onto the ticket price. For sought-after tickets, it's often a good idea to consult a helpful hotel porter who will do what he can to procure them (in return for a nice tip). Half-price tickets (plus a $1 or $2 service charge) can be bought for same-day performances from TKTS on *Times Square, West 47th Street/ Broadway; daily 15.00-20.00; tickets for matinée performances Wed and Sat from 12.00-14.00, Sun from 12.00-15.00.*

TIPPING

In New York, tips are not just appreciated, they are expected. Service is never included in the listed restaurant prices. Waiters should, therefore, receive a 15% tip. Head-waiters and *maitre d's* expect at least $10 for special services (such as arranging for a table by the window). In first-class restaurants, they would expect about $20. Bell-boys expect about $1 per piece of luggage, $5 in the smarter hotels. Chambermaids receive at least $5, or $1 per day for prolonged stays. Special services provided by the porter or the bell captain (such as booking tickets or tables at restaurants that are usually booked up) would usually set you back at least $10. Taxi drivers expect a minimum 15% tip.

TOURIST INFORMATION

Most of the individual states have representatives in all the major countries that should be able to supply basic tourist information. Alternatively, contact the U.S. Embassy in your country.

For general tourist information in the UK contact:
Visit USA Association
Tel: 0891 60 05 30
They operate a free brochure request line and will send you a selection of information on various U.S. destinations.

In New York:

New York Convention and Visitors Bureau   (105/E 6)
You can obtain the following information here free of charge: street maps, bus and subway maps,

Cruise the bay with the Seaport Line

a list of hotel prices, coming events and discount vouchers for theatre tickets. Information is only given on hotels, theatres or event-organizers that are members of the Bureau.

Mon-Fri 09.00-18.00; 224 West 42nd Street, between seventh and eighth Avenue, Tel: 484-1222; Internet: www. nycvisit.com; Subway: 42nd Str. 1, 2, 3, 9, N, R;

Travellers' Aid   (105/E 6)

An organization working with the police to assist victims of crime.

Mon-Fri, 09.00-17.00; Wed until 12.00; 1451 Broadway, corner 41st Street; Tel: 944-0013; Subway: 42nd Street/Times Square, 1, 2, 3, 7, 9, N, R. Also has an office in the International Arrivals hall of John F. Kennedy Airport; Tel: (718) 656-4870

Bus tours

Gray Line of New York
Offers 17 different tours, including double-decker bus tours, 2 to 8 hours long; from $19. *900 8th Avenue, between 53rd and 54th Street; Tel: 397-2600*
Harlem Spirituals
Offers tours around Harlem. *Sun* trips include a visit to a Baptist church *($33)*; *Mon, Thurs and Sat* evening trips include a visit to a jazz club *($75)*. *1697 Broadway/53rd Street; Tel: 757-0425*
New York Double Decker Tours
Offer open-top bus tours uptown and downtown *($28)*. *350 5th Avenue, 45th Floor; Tel: 967-6008*

Boat trips

Circle Line Sightseeing Tours: three-hour boat trips around Manhattan

($20). Daily, every 60 mins (10.00-16.00); mid-March to end of December; Circle Line Plaza, West 42nd Street and Hudson River; Tel: 563-3200
Pioneer: Two-hour tours of the harbour aboard an 1885 schooner *($16). South Street Seaport, Pier 16 (Fulton and Hudson Street); Tel: 748-8786*

World Yacht cruises
Dinner cruises are worthwhile if you can get a table by the window so you can enjoy a perfect view of the moon beaming down on the Statue of Liberty *($67-$79).*
Depart between 18.00 and 19.00; Pier 81, West 41st Street and Hudson River; Tel: 630-8100; Subway: 23rd Street, C, E

Helicopter tours
Island Helicopter Corporation. 7 to 22 minute round trips *($44-$139). Heliport, East 34th Street/East River; Tel: 683-4575*

TRANSPORT

Bus and subway
The bus and subway services (200 bus routes and 463 subway stations) are well interconnected. Obtain a New York Metropolitan Transportation Authority map free of charge from subway stations and you shouldn't have any difficulty getting around.

Note that normal trains are called *local trains*; some stations have separate entrances for up-town and downtown trains; *express trains* only stop at roughly every fifth station.

The subway fare is paid with tokens, which can only be bought from subway station ticket offices. The cost of a one-way trip is $1.50. Tokens are also valid on buses,

but bus fares can be paid in cash as well (coins only). If you need to catch a connecting bus, ask the driver for a 'transfer' ticket. One can transfer from the subway to the bus (or vice versa) using the new metro cards, which are available at subway stations and from kiosks and delis.

Limousines
There are a number of chauffeured limousine services in New York. A town car that seats three people costs around $50 a day to rent, and a stretch limo costs approximately $60 per hour (minimum: two hours). There is no extra charge for car phones (but the charge per unit is high), TV and bar. 20% tip. A reliable firm is: *Farrell Limousine Service; Tel: 988-4441.*

Car hire
If you want to hire a car in New York, you should do so at the airport as it's cheaper there than in Manhattan. You can get an even better rate if you book in advance through one of the larger firms (Avis, Hertz, Budget). In view of the very limited parking space on the streets and the high rate of car crime, you're well advised to use the multi-storey carparks (daily charge around $25).

Taxis
The official *Yellow Cabs* are not particularly expensive. The basic charge for the first fifth of a mile is $2, with an additional 30c for each subsequent fifth of a mile. Twenty-five blocks costs approximately $6.50 plus tip (15%). Evening supplement (after 20.00): 50c. Be prepared to pay toll fees for some bridges and

tunnels. Taxi ranks are confined to airports and stations, the Port Authority Bus Terminal and the large hotels (e.g. the Hilton).

WEATHER

The weather in New York can be extreme. The winters are bitter cold and the summers (from mid-June to mid-September) are hot and sticky, with temperatures climbing as high as 35°C (95°F). It's very easy to catch a cold as you pass from air-conditioned buildings to the hot, sweaty streets (for restaurants etc. it's a good idea always to take along a light jacket). Weatherwise, the best times to visit New York are from May to mid-June and from mid-September to the end of October.

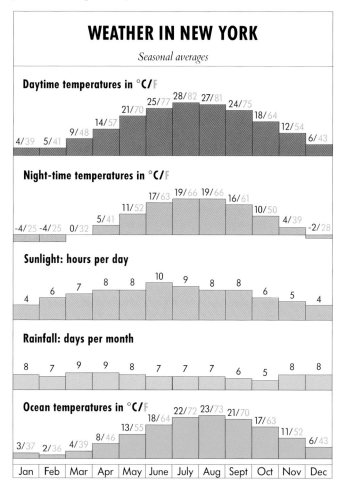

WEATHER IN NEW YORK

Seasonal averages

Daytime temperatures in °C/F

Jan	Feb	Mar	Apr	May	June	July	Aug	Sept	Oct	Nov	Dec
4/39	5/41	9/48	14/57	21/70	25/77	28/82	27/81	24/75	18/64	12/54	6/43

Night-time temperatures in °C/F

| -4/25 | -4/25 | 0/32 | 5/41 | 11/52 | 17/63 | 19/66 | 19/66 | 16/61 | 10/50 | 4/39 | -2/28 |

Sunlight: hours per day

| 4 | 6 | 7 | 8 | 8 | 10 | 9 | 8 | 8 | 6 | 5 | 4 |

Rainfall: days per month

| 8 | 7 | 9 | 9 | 8 | 7 | 7 | 7 | 6 | 5 | 8 | 8 |

Ocean temperatures in °C/F

| 3/37 | 2/36 | 4/39 | 8/46 | 13/55 | 18/64 | 22/72 | 23/73 | 21/70 | 17/63 | 11/52 | 6/43 |

Jan	Feb	Mar	Apr	May	June	July	Aug	Sept	Oct	Nov	Dec

Do's and don'ts

Some of the dangers and tourist traps
to watch out for in New York

Celebrity non-appearances!

There are a number of restaurants that will lure you in with the false hope that you will spot one or two stars. Signed photographs of celebrities with words of praise for the establishment hang in practically every pizzeria. Sardi's (which has 'the worst food in New York' according to food critic Tim Zagat), Gallagher's Steak House or any restaurant feeding people by the coachload are best avoided. Similarly, bars such as Michael's Pub (where Woody Allen supposedly goes on a Monday night to play clarinet) are not recommended. You have a better chance of running into Liza Minnelli or Sean Penn shopping on Columbus Avenue or of seeing Madonna or Woody Allen going for a morning walk in Central Park.

Healthy eating

Salad bars in delicatessens or self-service restaurants are popular, but be aware that a public health warning has been issued by the New York health authorities which advises that uncovered prepared food can harbour disease-carrying bacteria.

Jet lag

Try not to give in too easily to jet lag on your arrival in New York. When you have crossed several time zones over a relatively short period, your body will need some time to readjust. If you fly from Europe to the east coast of America, for example, it usually takes about three days to completely adjust. When you arrive (if you fly from Europe, it will always be in the afternoon New York time), it is recommended that you try and stave off – for a few hours at least – the temptation to crash into bed. If you go to sleep straight away, your internal clock function is likely to wake you some time in the early hours. Even if you do go to bed late, however, you won't always be able to shake off the fatigue. But should you wake up at the crack of dawn, don't worry – there's plenty to do in New York at 5 or 6 am. You could visit the fish or meat markets, have early-morning coffee in a corner shop or watch a little early morning TV in true American style. Experienced long-haul flyers arm themselves against the effects of jet lag as soon as they get on the plane. By drinking plenty of mineral water (at least a litre), you can counteract the effects of the aircraft's air-conditioning system, which dries out your body's natural moisture.

Photographic and electronics shops

Shops on Fifth Avenue with signs which say 'Going out of business' seldom actually close down. What's more, you can rarely find a bargain in them. It's always a good idea to compare different prices before parting with your money. Avoid buying pre-recorded video cassettes. They have probably been recorded from American television NTSC and are not compatible with PAL or SECAM.

Tax lies

The 8.25 % sales tax in New York will not be refunded on leaving the country despite what traders looking for a way to force up their prices will have you believe.

Taxi pirates

Unauthorized drivers with 'taxi' signs may try and offer you their services at the airport or in front of your hotel. They are seldom insured and usually charge astro-

nomical fares. You're strongly advised not to use them. The same applies if you're in town. Be careful of dubious taxi's that stop, offering you a limousine service. New Yorkers may use these so-called gypsy cabs, but they know how to negotiate the right price and can usually assess the situation from experience.

Theft and muggings

Try not to carry much more than $20 cash around with you, avoid opening your wallet/purse on the street and don't wear any valuable jewellery. Handbags should be hung across the body and not just on one shoulder.

A common mugger's ploy is to draw people into conversation to distract their attention while a partner in crime commits the actual theft.

Don't use the subway in the evenings after the rush hour or at night and don't walk in parks or deserted streets at night. The Bronx and Harlem should be visited only on a guided tour or in the company of someone who knows their way around. The same applies for certain parts of Manhattan (Washington Heights, the Bowery and Alphabet City on the Lower East Side).

No smoking

The smoking laws have become strict: smoking is forbidden on internal American flights, in trains, buses, banks and public buildings. This is now also true of large restaurants. America is turning into a non-smoking nation. Visitors must adapt. Simultaneous developments: classy, stylish cigar bars (e.g. Club Macanudo, Lexington Bar & Books, City Wine & Cigar Co.) and tour guides for smokers ('Smoking and Dining in Manhattan' by Kato Enterprises).

STREET ATLAS LEGEND

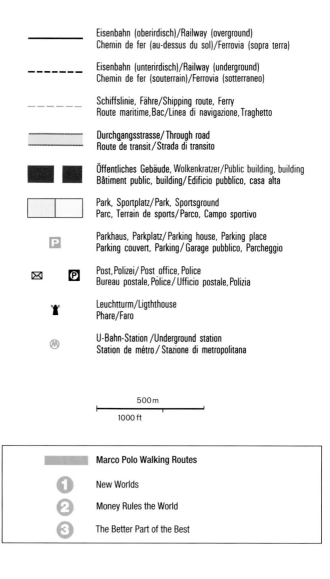

Eisenbahn (oberirdisch)/Railway (overground)
Chemin de fer (au-dessus du sol)/Ferrovia (sopra terra)

Eisenbahn (unterirdisch)/Railway (underground)
Chemin de fer (souterrain)/Ferrovia (sotterraneo)

Schiffslinie, Fähre/Shipping route, Ferry
Route maritime, Bac/Linea di navigazione, Traghetto

Durchgangsstrasse/Through road
Route de transit/Strada di transito

Öffentliches Gebäude, Wolkenkratzer/Public building, building
Bâtiment public, building/Edificio pubblico, casa alta

Park, Sportplatz/Park, Sportsground
Parc, Terrain de sports/Parco, Campo sportivo

Parkhaus, Parkplatz/Parking house, Parking place
Parking couvert, Parking/Garage pubblico, Parcheggio

Post, Polizei/Post office, Police
Bureau postale, Police/Ufficio postale, Polizia

Leuchtturm/Ligthhouse
Phare/Faro

U-Bahn-Station /Underground station
Station de métro / Stazione di metropolitana

500 m

1000 ft

	Marco Polo Walking Routes
1	New Worlds
2	Money Rules the World
3	The Better Part of the Best

Street Atlas of New York

*Please refer to back cover for an overview
of this street atlas*

A

B

C

1

2

3

4

5

6

Hudson River →

Riverside Drive

Hudson Parkway

Henry

Riverside

Park

Riverside

West

West

Wes

We:

Wes

Wes

Wes

Wes

Wes

Wes

Hive
Mus

W.

West

West

West

West

W.

Wes

Wes

West

West

West

Wes

Wes

West

West

West

West

West

West

West

West

West

Wes
R

We:

We:

Wes

West

Parkway

Hudson

Drive

Soldiers &
Sailors'
Monument

Jewish Martyrs
Memorial

W

Harbor
Dr.

Marine

Road

77th St.

GUTTENBERG

Boat Basin

Henry

Riverside

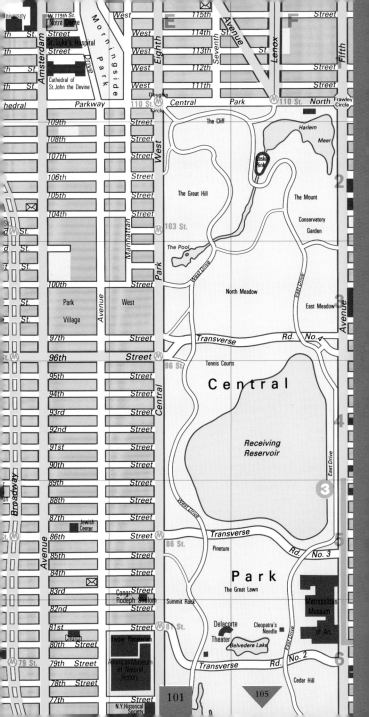

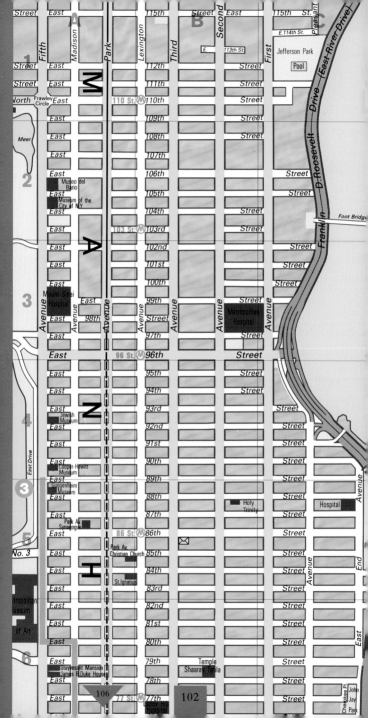

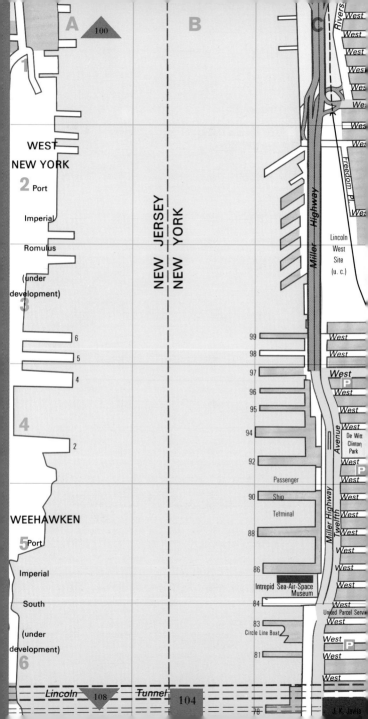

A
△ 100

B

C

Rivers | West

West

West

Wes

Wes

We:

We:

Wes

We:

**WEST
NEW YORK**

2 Port

Imperial

Romulus

(under

development)

3

Miller Highway

Freedom Pl.

Lincoln
West
Site
(u. c.)

We:

6

5

4

2

WEEHAWKEN

5 Port

Imperial

South

(under

development)

6

99

98

97

96

95

94

92

Passenger

90 Ship

Terminal

88

86

Intrepid Sea-Air-Space
Museum

84

83
Circle Line Boat

81

West

West

West | P

West

West

West | De Witt
Clinton
Park

West | P

West

West

West

West

West

West

West
United Parcel Servi

West

West | P

West

West

Twelfth Avenue

Miller Highway

J. K. Javits

Lincoln Tunnel (Toll)

J. K. Javits
Exhibition
and
Convention
Center

1

New Jersey Transit and
Amtrak Tunnels

76

73

West

72

West 30th St.
Heliport

West

2

Lincoln
Harbor

West

67

West

West

West

West

64

Wes

Boulevard

Twelfth

Avenue

3

7

6

5

4

3

2

1

62

61

Viaduct St.

13th Street

60

12th
Street
Hudson

Washington
ST.

Bloomfield

Garden

11th

59

58

4

1

2

3

4

57

Elysian
Park

Castle

Point

Ter.

Sinatra

56

10th

Street

Park

9th

Street

Willow

8th

Street

7th

Street

7

HOBOKEN

6th

Street

Drive

C

Hudson
Park

River

5th

Street

Church
Sq. Park

B

Clinton

4th

Street

Grand

Avenue

3rd

Street

Street

A

Hudson River

Rail Road and
Tunnels

54th Street
55th Street

Newton

Street

1st Street

Street

107

Paidge Ave.

St

Mc Guinness

Ash
Box
Street

Commercial

Clay

Manhattan

Provost
Street

Street
Street

Street
Street

Dupont

Franklin

Clay

Boulevard

West

Eagle

Street

Freeman

Green

Huron

Green

India

GREENPOINT

Street

Greenpoint Av.
M

Street

India

Java

Kent

Greenpoint

Street

Street

Milton

Street

Street

Noble

Oak

Calyer

Street

3

Street

Quai

e and
ort

oosevelt Drive

Bushwick Creek

East

John J Murphy
Park
E 16th St.

River

North 12th

North 11th

2

North 10th

WILLIAMS

East 15th St.

Street

Street

Haven
Plaza

Jacob
Rijs
Houses

N 9th

N 8th

N 7th

9th Street

St

Village
East
Towers

Street

East

8th Street

Jacob
Rijs
Houses

N 6th

5th

BURG

River

North

3rd

5th Street

Lillian

Metropolitan

North

1st

Wald Houses

Grand

Street

Wythe

Street

Wythe

Hamilton
Fish Park

ER

Street

Street

Street

N 4th

Columbia

Baruch

Baruch

S 2nd

6

Masaryk

Baruch Houses

111

115

South

5t

Bridge

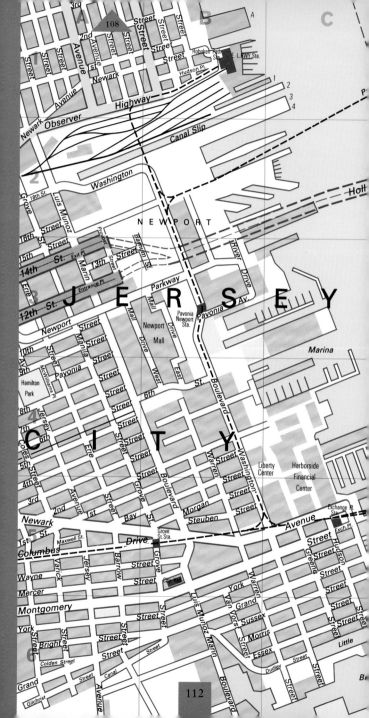

This index lists a selection of the streets and squares shown in the street atlas

116

118

24th St **103/F3; 107/F4-F1**
25th Rd **103/F4**
26th Ave **103/D4-F4**
26th Rd **103/F4**
27th Ave **103/E4-F4**
27th Rd **103/F4**
27th St **107/F3-F2**
28th Ave **103/E4-F4**
29th Ave **103/F4**
30th Ave **103/E5-F5**
30th Dr **103/E5-F5**
30th Rd **103/E5-F5**
31st Dr **103/E5-F6**
31st Rd **103/E5-F5**
31th Ave **103/E5-F5**
33rd Ave **103/E6-F6**
34th Ave **103/E6-F6**
35th Ave **107/E1-F1**
36th Ave **107/E1-F1**
37th Ave **107/E2-F2**
38th Ave **107/E2-F2**
39th Ave **107/F2**
40th Ave **107/E2-F3**
41st Ave **107/E3-F3**
41st Rd **107/E3**
42nd Rd **107/F3**
43rd Ave **107/E4-F4**
43rd Rd **107/E4**
44th Ave **107/E4-F4**
44th Rd **107/E4-F4**
44th St **107/F4**
45th Ave **107/E4-F4**
45th Dr **107/E4-F4**
45th Rd **107/E5-F4**
46th Ave **107/E5-F5**
46th Rd **107/E5-F5**
47th Ave **107/E5-F5**
47th Rd **107/E5-F5**
48th Ave **107/E6-E5**
49th Ave **107/E6-F5**
50th Ave **107/E6-F5**
51st Ave **107/E6-F6**
54th St **111/E1**
55th St **111/E1**
56th St **111/D1-E1**
Ash St **111/E1-F1**
Astoria Blvd **103/E4-F4**
Astoria Park South **103/E3-F3**
Borden Ave **107/E6-F6**
Box St **111/E1-F1**
Bridge Plaza North **107/E3-F3**
Bridge Plaza South **107/E3-F3**
Broadway **103/E6-F6**
Calyer St **111/F3**
Clay St **111/E1-F1**
Commercial St **111/E2-E1**
Court Sq **107/F4**
Crane St **107/F5**
Crescent St **103/F4-107/F4**
Davis St **107/F5**
Ditmars Blvd **103/F1**
Dupont St **111/E2-F1**
Eagle St **111/E2-F1**
Franklin St **111/E2-F3**
Freeman St **111/E2-F1**
Grand St **111/F6**
Green St **111/E2-F1**

Greenpoint Ave **111/F3-F2**
Hell Gate Bridge **103/E2-F2**
Hoyt Ave North **103/F3**
Hoyt Ave South **103/F3**
Hunter St **111/F4-F3**
Huron St **111/E2-F1**
India St **111/E2-F1**
Jackson Ave **107/F5-F4**
Java St **111/E2-F2**
Kent Ave **111/F4-F6**
Kent St **111/E3-F2**
MacGuiness Blvd **111/F1-F2**
Main Ave **111/E5-E4**
Manhattan Ave **111/E1-F2**
Metropolitan Ave **111/F5**
Milton St **111/F3-F2**
Noble St **111/F3-F2**
North 1st St **111/F5**
North 3rd St **111/F5**
North 4th St **111/F5**
North 5th St **111/F5**
North 11th St **111/F4**
North 12th St **111/F4**
Oak St **111/F3**
Paidge Ave **111/F1**
Pearson St **107/F4-F5**
Provost St **111/F1**
Pulaski Bridge **107/F6**
Quai St **111/F3**
River St **111/F6-F5**
Shore Blvd **103/F2-F1**
Skillman Ave **107/F5**
South 1st St **111/F6**
South 2nd St **111/F6**
South 3rd St **111/F6**
South 4th St **111/F6**
South 5th St **111/F6**
Thomson Ave **107/F4**
Triborough Bridge **103/D1-F3**
Vernon Blvd **103/E5-107/E6**
Welling St **103/E5**
West St **111/E2-F3**
Wythe Ave **111/F5-F6**

CITY OF HOBOKEN
1st St **112/A1-B1**
2nd St **112/A1-B1**
3rd St **108/A6**
4th St **108/A6**
5th St **108/A6**
6th St **108/A6-A5**
7th St **108/A5**
8th St **108/A5**
9th St **108/A5**
10th St **108/A4-A5**
11th St **108/A4**
12th St **108/A4**
13th St **108/A4**
Bloomfield St **108/A4-112/A1**
Castle Point Terrace **108/A4-A5**
Garden St **108/A4-112/A1**
Hudson Pl **112/B1**
Hudson St **108/A3-112/B1**
Newark Ave **112/A1-A2**
Newark St **112/A1-B1**
Observer Highway **112/A1-B1**
Park Ave **108/A4-112/B2**

River St **108/B6-112/B1**
Sinatra Dr **108/A4-B6**
Washington St **108/A4-112/B1**
Willow Ave **108/A5-112/B2**

JERSEY CITY
1st St **112/A5-B4**
2nd St **112/A5-B4**
3rd St **112/A5-B4**
4th St **112/A5-A4**
5th St **112/A4**
6th St **112/A4-B4**
7th St **112/A4**
8th St **112/A4**
9th St **112/A4-A3**
10th St **112/A3**
12th St **112/A3**
13th St **112/A3**
14th St **112/A3**
15th St **112/A3-A2**
16th St **112/A2**
18th St **112/A2**
Barnum St **112/A3-B3**
Barrow St **112/A5-A6**
Bay St **112/A5-B4**
Bright St **112/A6**
Canal St **112/A6-B6**
Chr. Columbus Dr **112/A5-B5**
Colden St **112/A6**
Dudley St **112/B6-C6**
Entrance Pl **112/A3**
Erie St **112/A3-A5**
Essex St **112/B6-C6**
Exchange Pl **112/C5**
Exit Pl **112/A3**
Gilchrist St **112/A6**
Grand St **112/A6-C5**
Greene St **112/C5-C6**
Grove St **112/A2-B6**
Hudson St **112/C5-C6**
Jersey Ave **112/A4-A6**
Luis Munoz Marin Blvd **112/A2-B6**
Mall Dr East **112/B3-B4**
Mall Dr West **112/A3-B4**
Manila St **112/A3-A4**
Maxwell St **112/A5**
McWilliams Pl **112/A4**
Mercer St **112A5-B5**
Montgomery St **112/A6-C5**
Morgan St **112/B5**
Morris St **112/B6-C6**
Newark Ave **112/A5-C5**
Newport Pkwy **112/A3-B3**
Pavonia Ave **112/B3**
Pavonia St **112/A4**
Provost St **112/A2-A3**
River Dr **112/B3**
Steuben St **112/B5**
Sussex St **112/B6-C5**
Van Vorst St **112/B6**
Varick St **112/A5-A6**
Warren St **112/B4-C6**
Washington Blvd **112/A2-B4**
Washington St **112/B4-C6**
Wayne St **112/A5-B5**
York St **112/A6-C5**

This index lists all the main sights, museums and theatres mentioned in this guide. The page number for the main entry is in boldface. Page numbers in italics refer to illustrations.

What do you get for your money?

 The dollar used to be the reserve currency, but over the last few years the exchange rate has been far from steady.

Here are a few examples of prices the tourist may expect to find in New York: you can buy an American coffee in a coffee shop for around 95c a cup, a cappuccino in one of the many espresso bars for $4. A small beer in a bar costs $3, a plain hamburger $8. A trip through Central Park in a horse and cart costs $34.

Local telephone calls are 25c, speaking to Europe for one minute will amount to $1.77. If you're sending postcards, you can count on about 30c for the card and a further 50c for the stamp.

Admiring the view of the world below from the 107th floor of the World Trade Center will cost you $10. Shoeshiners in the street ask $3 for their services.

Cinema tickets cost $8, tickets for a Broadway musical will cost approximately $60. A pair of Levi's 501 jeans cost $47 at the Original Levi's Store on 57th Street.

 Credit cards are accepted in nearly every restaurant and hotel in New York as well as in most shops. Travellers cheques are universally accepted, but Eurocheques are not recognized.

US $	UK £	Can $
1	0.59	1.55
2	1.18	3.10
3	1.77	4.65
4	2.36	6.20
5	2.95	7.75
10	5.90	15.50
15	8.85	32.25
20	11.80	31.00
30	17.70	46.50
40	23.60	62.00
50	29.50	77.50
60	35.40	93.00
70	41.30	108.50
80	47.20	124.00
90	53.10	139.50
100	59.00	155.00
200	118.00	310.00
300	177.00	465.00
400	236.00	620.00
500	295.00	775.00
750	442.50	1162.50
1000	590.00	1550.00